Photography

AN ILLUSTRATED HISTORY

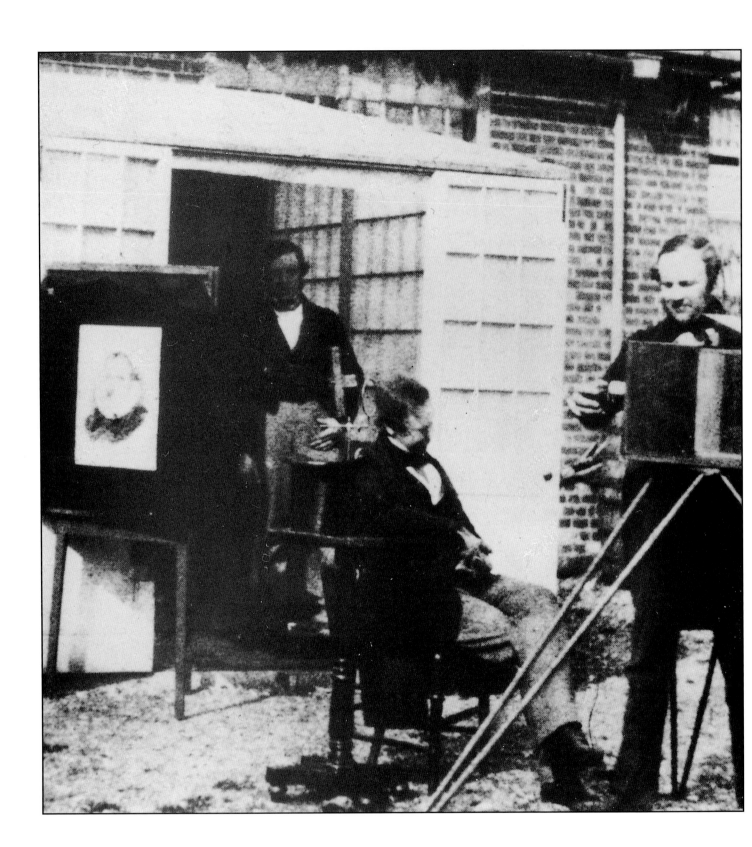

Photography

An Illustrated History

Martin W. Sandler

OXFORD

UNIVERSITY PRESS

OXFORD
UNIVERSITY PRESS

Oxford   New York
Athens Auckland Bangkok Bogotá Buenos Aires Cape Town
Chennai Dar es Salaam Delhi Florence Hong Kong Istanbul Karachi
Kolkata Kuala Lumpur Madrid Melbourne Mexico City Mumbai Nairobi
Paris São Paulo Shanghai Singapore Taipei Tokyo Toronto Warsaw

and associated companies in   Berlin   Ibadan

Copyright © 2002 by Martin W. Sandler
Published by Oxford University Press, Inc.
198 Madison Avenue, New York, New York 10016
www.oup.com

Oxford is a registered trademark of Oxford University Press

Design: Sandy Kaufman
Layout: Loraine Machlin

Library of Congress Cataloging-in-Publication Data available

ISBN 0-19-512608-4

1 3 5 7 9 8 6 4 2

Printed in Hong Kong
on acid-free paper

On the cover: William Henry Jackson photographing Yosemite Falls, around 1880.

Frontispiece: The first commercial photographic printing establishment, operated by William Henry Fox Talbot in Reading, England, in 1846.

Title page: Russell Lee. A crowd in front of a traveling photographer's tent, 1938.

Contents page: Dr. Harold Edgerton. *Flying bullet,* 1964.

Contents

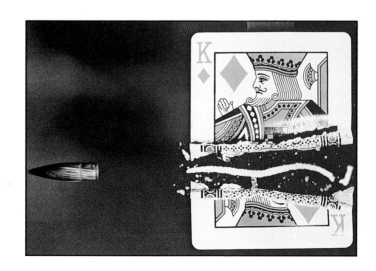

Chapter One
Beginnings

A photograph is a kind of miracle. There is a picture of our mother exactly as she looked as a child. There, in another picture, is a scene of an event that helped shape the history of a nation, taken at the moment it happened. There, in yet another image, is a photograph created so artistically that it is a profound delight to see.

When photography burst upon the scene in the first half of the 19th century, people were amazed by the fact that they were suddenly able to view or even possess an exact likeness of themselves, their relatives, their friends, and the celebrities of their day. Looking back at that time, what is equally amazing is how rapidly the medium of photography advanced. Within only 50 years of its introduction, photographers not only had the ability to capture likenesses but were recording places and events around the world. They also had the means and the skill to produce photographs that were regarded as works of art.

The first official forms of photography were the daguerreotype and the calotype, or talbotype, as it was also called. They appeared in 1839 and 1841, but there had been an earlier achievement in recording a permanent image in a camera. In 1827, a French engineer and experimenter, Joseph Nicephore Niépce, had produced a small, crude but permanent positive image on a metal plate. However, his method did not use light-sensitive silver compounds, which are the basis of photography, and required an eight-hour exposure. It was far from being a practical process.

The daguerreotype was named after its inventor, the Frenchman Louis Jacques Mandé Daguerre. His achievement was announced in January 1839 but was shown only to small invited audiences until August of that year, when Daguerre gave a public demonstration of the procedures. The calotype was invented by an Englishman, William Henry Fox Talbot, who showed some images and described a preliminary version of his process just three weeks after Daguerre made his accomplishment known, but he did not perfect it and release the details for another year and a half.

The calotype had much more importance for the future development of photography, but the daguerreotype produced far more beautiful, and technically perfect,

Frederick Fargo Church. *George Eastman with a Kodak Camera on Board the* S. S. Gallia, 1890.

In 1888, George Eastman invented a small, easy-to-use camera that made it possible for almost everyone to take pictures. Here, Eastman demonstrates his invention aboard an ocean liner.

images and was the dominant method for the first 15 years of the medium. Thus, for his invention of the first practical method of recording images in a camera, Daguerre is recognized as the father of photography.

In order for photography (the word means "writing with light") to be invented, two elements were necessary. One was an optical and mechanical device for forming an image. The other was a chemical procedure for making a permanent record of the image. The optical principles of forming a visual image had been known for thousands of years. By the mid 16th century, astronomers and artists were using a device based on those principles, called a *camera obscura* ("dark chamber") to view eclipses and other sun phenomena and to make drawings. The first camera obscuras were literally dark rooms. They operated on the principle that if a small hole is made in a wall of a darkened room, an upside down and left-right reversed image of the outside view in front of the hole will appear inside, on the opposite wall. A person inside the room could then trace the image on paper. By the late 17th century, a portable box-shaped camera obscura with an image-forming lens in place of a hole had been perfected and was commonly used by artists for tracing images of real scenes and objects. Thus, the camera was in existence at least 250 years before a chemical procedure for recording its images permanently on some kind of surface was invented. Daguerre and Talbot both solved the image-recording problem by experimenting with light-sensitive silver compounds, but their results were very different.

To make a photograph, Daguerre used a highly polished, silver-plated sheet of copper. He treated the silver surface with fumes from heated crystals of iodine to make it light sensitive and exposed it to the focused image in a camera obscura. This formed an invisible *latent image* on the plate. To make the latent image visible—*develop* it—he treated the silver plate with fumes from heated mercury. Development brought out the very light and middle-tone areas of the image in proportion to their brightness in the scene. In this way, a *direct*

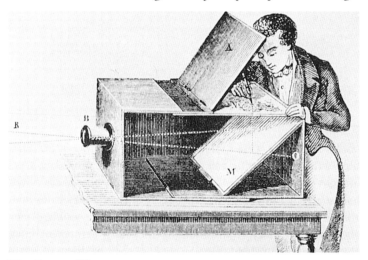

The Camera Obscura
The portable camera obscura provided the optical element necessary for photography. It was constructed with a lens at one end of a long wooden box. A mirror placed inside the box at a 45-degree angle reflected the image from the lens upward to a sheet of glass placed flush with the top of the box. A lens forms an image that is upside down and reversed left for right. The mirror reflection turned the image right side up but did not correct the left-right reversal. To use the camera obscura, an artist would place a thin piece of paper on the glass to view or trace the image. Cloth baffles (not shown) on each side of the lid over the glass blocked stray light that would wash out the projected image.

An early photographer retouches one of his daguerreotypes. Among those who were astounded by the earliest form of photography was the English poet Elizabeth Barrett Browning. "I would rather have [a daguerreotype] of one I dearly loved," she wrote, "than the noblest artist's work ever produced."

positive image, not a negative, appeared. To make the picture permanent, or *fix* it, he bathed the plate in a solution of hyposulfite of soda, which made the unexposed, undeveloped parts of the plate no longer light sensitive. (The same fixing chemical is used with both black-and-white and color films and prints today. It is now named sodium thiosulfate, but still called "hypo" by many photographers.) Finally, he washed the plate in water.

Most daguerreotypes were 3 1/4 by 4 1/4 inches in size (larger sizes were made, but silver plates were quite expensive). The image was "as delicate as the pattern on a butterfly's wing," one early observer noted. To protect it, a brass mat with a cutout to reveal the image was placed over the plate and then a glass cover was added. These were held together with a thin brass frame around the edges, and the packet was fitted into a small booklike case with velvet or silk padding in the hinged cover.

Because of its mirrorlike silver surface, a daguerreotype had to be held at an angle away from direct light, reflecting something dark. Then its lustrous silvery and white tones shone as if they were light themselves, revealing the most delicate changes in brightness and shade. People marveled at the reality and clarity of the images, which had none of the sand-particle pattern, called graininess, sometimes seen in prints enlarged from small negatives today. They were even more amazed when they looked at them through a magnifying glass, which revealed more and more, increasingly finer detail. The leaves on individual distant trees, the tiles on a roof several blocks away were clear and sharp.

Never one for modesty, Daguerre gave the name *daguerreotype* to the photographs his process produced. The French government gave Daguerre several thousand francs and a lifetime pension for the rights to his invention, in order to present the process free to the world as a philanthropic demonstration of France's superiority in science. In August 1839, Daguerre himself gave the demonstration that made the process public. The event was attended by the entire French legislature, scientists and dignitaries of all kinds, hundreds of ordinary citizens, and newspaper reporters from every major city in the world. At the same time he published a manual of the process, the first book on photographic technique ever written.

Daguerre also patented an improved box-size camera obscura for taking daguerreotypes. The lens was covered by a thin metal

William Henry Fox Talbot.
Leaves of Orchidea, 1839.

Before producing photographs through his calotype process, Talbot created photogenic drawings by placing objects like these orchid leaves on a sheet of paper soaked in silver nitrate or chloride. The image appeared after the paper was placed in the sunlight for 10 to 30 minutes.

plate that pivoted out of the way to let light pass through. This shutter (a literal name—it opened and shut the lens) was operated by hand. No mechanism was needed, because exposure times ranged from 20 to 45 minutes or longer, depending on the time of day and season of the year. By 1841, a variety of daguerreotype cameras were being produced in France, Germany, Austria, and the United States. Because the daguerreotype was a direct positive process, a photographer had to expose a separate plate for each copy of a picture he wanted.

William Henry Fox Talbot's photographic process, the *calotype,* allowed duplicate copies—prints—to be made. When all previous experimenters had obtained an image in which the light and dark areas were the reverse of their brightness in the actual subject—a negative image—they thought it was a mistake and a failure. Talbot's great insight was to recognize that the negative was just an intermediate step, and that by exposing another piece of sensitized material to this "mistake" the lights and darks would be reversed again to their normal appearance. This was a *negative–positive* process, the foundation for every improved photographic method to come.

Talbot used high-quality writing paper rather than a metal plate. Because it was 100 percent cotton fiber ("rag") paper, it did not wrinkle or disintegrate when dampened, as later wood-pulp papers do. He treated the paper with solutions of silver nitrate, potassium iodide, and gallic acid to make it light sensitive, and exposed it while still damp in a camera obscura. He developed the latent image with a silver nitrate and gallic acid solution, and. made the visible image permanent with a solution of hyposulfite of soda, followed by washing.

The developed image was a negative. To make a positive print, Talbot placed the negative against a piece of similarly sensitized paper and exposed this sandwich, clamped in a kind of picture frame, to sunlight. When he judged the strength of the tones to be right, Talbot fixed the paper in a hypo solution so that light would no longer affect it, and washed it in water. Finally, for support, the thin paper was mounted on a card or thicker paper.

The final image, the positive print, was quite different from a daguerreotype. Its tones were brown, not shades of gray and black as in modern prints. The details of the print were not razor sharp, partly because the image was formed in the fibers of the paper, not in a smooth coating on top of the surface, and partly because the fibers of the paper negative interfered with the exposing light. This lack of sharpness in detail gave the finished calotype an overall appearance similar to that of a fine engraving or etching, a quality that many early photographers found appealing.

The Camera

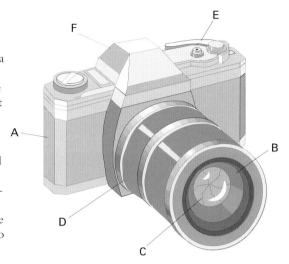

From the beginnings of photography, there have been thousands of different types of cameras. But whether old or new, large or small, almost all cameras have the same fundamental features.

These features include: (A) A lightproof chamber, which allows only the light from the lens to reach the glass plate or film on which the image is recorded. (B) A lens, a combination of shaped pieces of optical glass or plastic that focuses light from the subject or scene in front of the camera onto the plate or film inside. (C) An iris diaphragm, a set of curved blades in the lens that form an adjustable-size hole called an aperture. Changing the size of the aperture changes the amount of light passing through the lens and therefore is one of the two ways of controlling the amount of exposure the film receives. Settings for various aperture sizes are marked on the lens by a series of f-numbers or "f-stops." Each larger aperture setting doubles the amount of light transmitted; each smaller aperture cuts it in half. (D) A shutter that opens and closes to control the length of time the image from the lens exposes the film. It is either a set of spring-driven blades, like an iris diaphragm, built into the lens, or is a curtain or set of blades located just in front of the film. The speed at which the shutter opens and closes—usually a fraction of a second—is controlled by a setting ring on the lens or a dial on the camera body, or by internal circuitry in cameras with automatic exposure control. The combination of shutter speed and aperture size determines the amount of exposure the film receives. If it is too little, the film will be *underexposed* and the picture will be too dark. If the film receives too much exposure—is *overexposed*—the picture will be too light. (E) The film advance, which on most modern cameras is automatic, may also appear as a manual knob or dial advance. (F) A viewfinder system, which permits the camera's user to see the subject area and compose the picture. It may be an optical viewer on top that shows the subject directly or a screen in the rear or top of the camera that shows the actual image the lens is projecting toward the film.

Talbot's first cameras were quite small wooden boxes—his wife called them "mousetraps"—and the images were about the size of a large postage stamp. Each "mousetrap" had a hole in the back with a pivoted brass cover so the photographer could view the image when he set up the camera. By the time Talbot perfected his process he was using cameras sized for larger images, with lenses that had pivoted shutter covers, like daguerreotype lenses. The cameras accepted removable paper holders and had a small inspection hole in the front that was plugged with a cork to keep light out when not used.

Talbot's name for his pictures, calotypes, came from the Greek word *kalos,* "beautiful." Friends urged him to call them Talbotypes, just as Daguerre had named his process for himself, and for a time both names were used. Although the process was essentially complete in 1839, Talbot did not publish a description of it until early 1841, and did not demonstrate it before the Royal Society, England's premiere scientific organization, of which he was a member, until later that year, after he had obtained a patent.

Although the negative-positive calotype process was to become the basis for almost all photography to follow, it was the beauty and amazing reality of the daguerreotype that had the greatest immediate impact, capturing the attention of people everywhere. From the very beginning, daguerreotypes were a sensation.

They became even more of a sensation when, in 1843, it became truly practical to

take portraits. The photographs people wanted most, then as now, were pictures of themselves, their friends, and the well-known and newsworthy individuals of the day. In every year since that time, hundreds of thousands, even millions, more pictures have been taken of people than of any other subject.

The earliest attempts to make daguerreotype portraits required subjects to sit perfectly still for almost 20 minutes in the full sun in order to expose a plate sufficiently. Their eyes would blink and water, the glare was almost unbearable, and to actually sit still that long was virtually impossible. By early 1843, improvements in the chemical mix used to sensitize the plate, and more important, a new kind of lens that transmitted over 16 times more light than the original daguerreotype lenses, made exposures of 5 to 30 seconds possible in full sunlight.

Almost overnight, daguerreotype studios sprang up all over the world. They became most popular in the United States, where the daguerreotype's greatest champion was

the inventor of the telegraph, Samuel F. B. Morse. When Daguerre's accomplishment was officially announced in 1839, Morse was in Paris to license the French rights to his invention. He demonstrated his telegraph to Daguerre, who in turn showed Morse how daguerreotypes were produced. Morse, who was primarily a portrait painter, was completely taken with the photographic discovery. When he returned to America he experimented with taking daguerreotypes, with the intention of getting reference images for use in his portrait painting. He also offered to teach the process to others. Among his pupils was Mathew B. Brady, who eventually became one of the most successful daguerreotypists of all.

In 1844, when he was only 21 years old, Brady opened his first photographic studio in New York, and between 1849 and 1860 he established three other photographic studios and galleries, one in Washington, D.C., and two more in New York. Each of these studios attracted many of the leading political figures and celebrities of the day, all anxious to have their portraits captured by Brady. Among these famous subjects were Daniel Webster, John Quincy Adams, Andrew Jackson, and a young Abraham Lincoln. From the beginning Brady daguerreotypes were widely acclaimed and earned several of the earliest photographic awards ever given. Although Brady himself actually took some pictures in the early years, he soon was fully involved in managing and promoting his establishments. The studio work was done by the several camera operators hired in each location. The credit line "Photograph by Brady" was a corporate credit, like

"Automobile by Ford"; it did not mean that Mathew Brady himself had taken the picture.

Taking a good-quality daguerreotype was not an easily learned skill. Because of the technicalities involved and the often lengthy exposure time required, almost all daguerreotypists concentrated on taking portraits—that was what people wanted to buy. There were some photographers, however, who packed up their cumbersome gear and took daguerreotypes of scenes away from their studios.

Perhaps the most accomplished of all these adventurous pioneer photographers was John Plumbe Jr. who emigrated to the United States from Wales in 1821. In 1840, after several years in railroad construction, he opened a daguerreotype studio in Washington, D.C., making him one of the first professional daguerreotype photographers in the United States. Shortly thereafter he opened a second studio in Boston. By the mid 1840s he had studios in other major cities in the United States and in Paris, France, and Liverpool, England. At the height of his business operations, some 500 people worked for him.

Plumbe himself was an excellent portraitist. The *New York Herald* referred to one of his daguerreotypes as "the most beautiful and finished portrait of the kind that we have ever looked upon." But his importance to the story of photography lies in the quality of the daguerreotypes that he took outside his studio.

In the mid 1840s, when Plumbe was operating in Washington, D.C., many of the buildings destined to become national landmarks had recently been built or were just being erected. Washington itself was rapidly becoming recognized as a city of great importance. Plumbe's daguerreotypes of such structures as the White House, the Patent Building, and the United States Capitol building, still under construction, gave Americans and many foreigners their first views of these symbols of a young nation on the rise. Today, his Washington images rank among the most prized of photographs, treasured not only by those interested in photography but of great value to architects and historians as well.

For the first 12 years of photography's existence, the daguerreotype and the calotype were the only significant forms of photography. Then, in 1851, an Englishman, Frederick Scott Archer, introduced a great improvement, the *collodion process.* Like the

John Plumbe Jr.'s 1846 daguerreotype of the Capitol of the United States under construction would have been lost to history had it not been discovered by a California photographic collector. In 1972 he found the daguerreotype in a flea market.

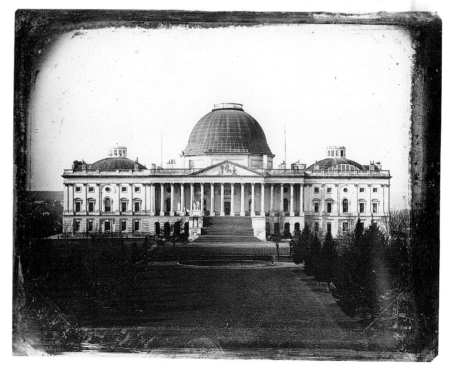

Timothy O'Sullivan. *Black Cañon of the Colorado,* 1871.

The early photographers of the American West were among the first to take their pictures with wet plates. One of the most successful of these photographers, O'Sullivan, captured this image at a point on the Colorado River. The small cloth-draped box in the boat was used as a portable darkroom so that the photographer could develop his images before the collodion on the wet plates dried.

calotype, it was a way of making negatives, but instead of paper it used glass plates.

Collodion was a gluey liquid. With potassium iodide crystals mixed in, it was poured in an even coating on a glass plate and made light sensitive in a silver nitrate bath. Because the coated plate had to be exposed and processed while still moist—within about 20 minutes in most situations—this means of capturing an image became commonly known as the *wet plate* process. If the plate dried too soon, the developer and other solutions could not act, because the collodion was then completely waterproof. This presented a major challenge to photographers. When they wanted to photograph outside the studio, they had to carry portable darkroom tents, chemicals, and other equipment with them so they could prepare and process their plates on the spot. In spite of this, photographers everywhere turned to the new process. For the next 30 years, the collodion-

covered glass plate would be the world's standard means of obtaining a photographic image.

The glass-plate negative produced the clearest, most tonally rich and sharply detailed prints yet made, especially when used with a new print material, *albumen paper,* introduced in 1850. This paper carried its image-forming crystals in a smooth surface coating of diluted egg whites (albumen). Printing was done in the same way as with the calotype but with a glass negative, which meant that no paper fibers interfered with the quality of the image: The negative plate was placed in contact with the print paper in a glass frame and exposed to sunlight until the image printed out to the proper intensity. Then it was fixed in hypo, washed, and mounted.

The collodion process not only made glass negatives possible but also spawned various other types of photography. One of these, the *ambrotype,* almost immediately

The tintype was one of the most popular forms of early photography. Many women wore lockets with tiny tintype images of loved ones inserted in them.

drove the daguerreotype out of existence. The negative image of a wet plate was composed of various densities of light gray particles, not black silver as in a modern negative. When placed on a black background, the image looked positive. Seizing on this phenomenon, portrait photographers began taking negatives on plates the same size as daguerreotype plates and painting the back side of the glass with black lacquer to make the image appear positive. Or they would simply place a piece of black cloth or paper behind the plate. Ambrotypes were matted and framed in padded cases just like daguerreotypes—but at a fraction of the cost. While only reasonably well-to-do customers could afford a daguerreotype, the ambrotype made portraits affordable to a much wider public, and studio business boomed.

The principle of a black background making a collodion negative look positive was exploited in another process, one that was so cheap to produce that even working-class families could afford to have pictures made. The process was officially named the *ferrotype* ("ferro" is a prefix meaning iron), for the pieces of thin sheet iron used in place of glass. However, the name almost everyone used was *tintype*, because the same kind of metal was coated with tin in making tin cans. Photographers purchased plates that were already lacquered black. They coated one side with collodion, sensitized, exposed, and processed it, and in no more than five minutes had a direct positive image.

Most tintypes were 2 1/2 by 4 inches, a size that could easily be sent through the mail, carried in the pocket, or kept in an album. To get more than just one image, a larger metal plate was used in a camera that had 4, 8, 12, or even 24 small lenses, each projecting a separate image on a section of the plate. A sliding shutter-panel opened or covered all the lenses at the same time, so every picture was the same. After processing, the images were cut apart with tin snips and the smallest were usually mounted on cards.

Because they were so inexpensive, tintypes were purchased in huge numbers and used for a wide variety of purposes. Traveling tintype "professors" set up their cameras at fairs, beaches, carnivals, and boardwalks. Miniature tintypes were used in cuff links, tie pins, and rings. Tintypes were cheap, quick to get, durable—and immensely popular.

Frances Benjamin Johnston, one of the first documentary photographers, sells tintypes at a country fair in 1903. The collodion process that made the tintype, the stereograph, and the wet plate possible revolutionized photography. "Photography," stated one British newspaper, "is everywhere now. Our truest friends, our most intimate enemies, stare us in the face from collodionized surfaces."

Alexander Gardner. Carte-de-visite of Walt Whitman, 1864.

"By giving infinitely more for infinitely less [Adolphe Disdéri] definitively popularized photography," wrote the photographer who went by the name Nadar. The subject of this carte-de-visite, American poet Walt Whitman, has autographed it, possibly as a gift.

The collodion process was also responsible for another form of picture that was introduced even earlier than the tintype. This type of photograph was produced in greater quantities and used for even more purposes. In 1854, a French portrait photographer, Adolphe Eugène Disdéri, patented the *carte-de-visite,* a name he gave both to the camera he invented and the pictures he took. The camera had four lenses and a sliding back that held a full-size plate (6 1/2 by 8 1/2 inches). Four pictures were exposed on one half of the plate by uncovering the lenses all together, or singly, or in pairs; then the plate was moved and four more exposures were made on the second half. After the processed negative was printed onto a single sheet of paper, the images were cut apart and mounted on individual cards.

In French, "carte de visite" means "visiting card." Disdéri used the same size card, 2 1/2 by 4 1/2 inches, to mount the pictures, and so gave them that name. But they were seldom used as visiting cards. Clothing and specialty stores used them in counter catalogs to show the range of goods they offered beyond what might be on display. Cartes were sold in the hundreds of thousands as souvenirs at popular tourist attractions and as novelties showing funny, strange, or foreign people, places, and things. Politicians distributed cartes during their campaigns, and celebrities used them for publicity. But far and away their major use for more than 50 years was for portraits.

Cartes cost only a few pennies each, and portrait customers would order multiple copies of poses they liked to give to family and friends. While we see primarily the rich and the upper middle class in daguerreo-

types and studio wet plate portraits, it is the tintype and the carte-de-visite, both produced in the millions, that show us ordinary middle-class families, workers of all sorts, athletes, soldiers—an ever-widening range of individuals. Then, as now, those images increased our knowledge and understanding of the people of the world.

Another outgrowth of the collodion process, the *stereograph,* had a profound effect in showing viewers the wonders and diversity of the physical world. For the public, the stereograph became the television of its day. It provided three-dimensional images of whatever the camera saw, because it effectively duplicated the way we actually look at an object. Each of our eyes sees an object from a slightly different angle. When those two images are relayed to our brain, a sense of depth or perspective is created. This phenomenon was understood well before photography was invented. Some artists drew pictures in pairs to achieve this stereo or three-dimensional effect. Some stereo daguerreotypes were even made. But it was the collodion process and a special camera that made it easy to obtain such images.

A stereographic camera had two lenses placed side by side, two and a half inches apart—the average distance between human eyes. Both lenses were opened at the same time and two images, identical except for the slight difference in angle of view, were recorded on the glass negative. Prints of these images were mounted on a horizontal card. When the card was placed in a hand-held device called a stereoscope, viewers could see the picture in three dimensions. Produced in enormous quantities, stereographs were sold through the

The author Oliver Wendell Holmes was so taken with the stereograph's ability to record exotic lands and peoples that he recommended the establishment of national and local stereographic libraries. This stereoscope, invented by Holmes, was lighter and easier to use than any of the other devices on the market and became the most popular model.

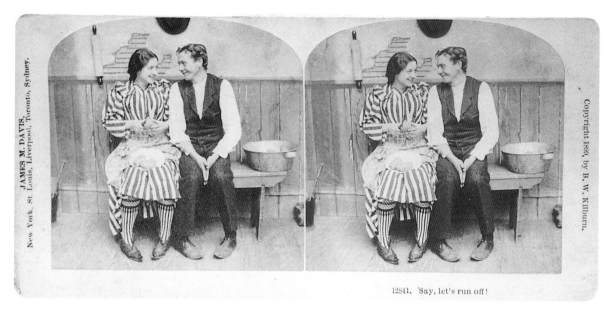

12841. 'Say, let's run off!

In the 1850s and 1860s stereoscopes and albums containing cards could be found in parlors of homes throughout the world. In an age before television and movies, humorous stereographs and charming stereos, such as this one of a lovesick couple, were extremely popular and sold by the thousands.

mail and from door to door as well in bookstores, stationers, and other outlets. Large companies devoted exclusively to the production of stereographs were formed and became highly successful.

For photographers, the stereograph opened up a whole new world of opportunity. Aware that their pictures could be widely sold, they traveled to even the most remote places to capture scenes they knew would appeal to a waiting public. For the public, the stereograph opened up whole new worlds as well. Through their stereoscopes, families viewed places they would be most unlikely ever to encounter in person—mountains, deserts, tropical jungles, ancient ruins, monuments such as the Sphinx, castles, cathedrals, foreign cities. They also saw people they would never meet—Indians on the American plains, newly arrived pioneers plowing up the virgin western soil, gold miners digging for riches in California and Alaska, railroad construction crews laying tracks through the wilderness. Printed text on the backs of the cards gave additional information about what was shown in the picture. The public was fascinated with this new medium of knowledge and bought sets of cards devoted to various topics, as well as individual cards.

Viewers also liked humorous scenes and pictures that illustrated well-known stories and poems. Stereograph producers staged and photographed such events in their studios. Series of pictures such as those depicting nervous bridegrooms attempting to flee from the church, farmers being chased by a bull, children playing pranks on each other, scenes from tales like "Little Red Riding Hood," and poems like "The Village Blacksmith" became a chief source of entertainment for millions of men, women, and children.

The major drawback of the collodion "wet plate" process was having to carry everything needed to prepare and process the plate on the spot. Photographers longed for a *dry* coating for their plates, and in 1871 they got it. A British physician, Richard Leach Maddox, demonstrated a new type of photographic plate.

Instead of collodion, Maddox used a layer of gelatin that contained light-sensitive crystals. This was the first true photographic *emulsion*. Once the gelatin dried, the plates could be taken anywhere for use and then brought back to the darkroom to be developed anytime the photographer desired. Not only were the dry plates far easier to handle than their sticky wet predecessors, they required less exposure time. Before long they could be purchased fully ready for use, usually in boxes of six or a dozen. These factors

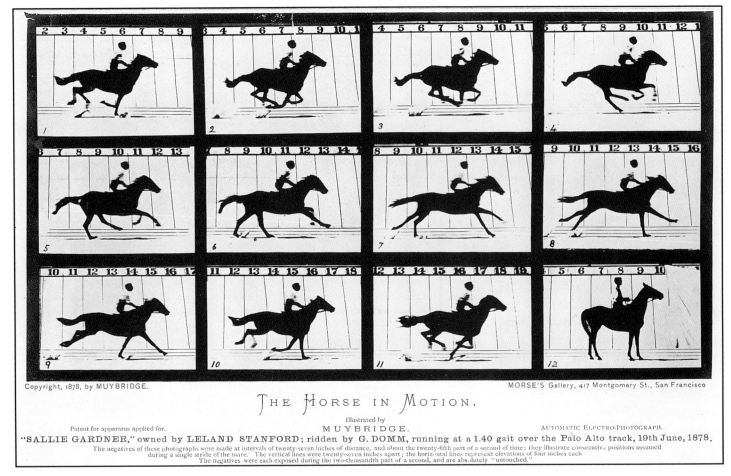

THE HORSE IN MOTION.

Illustrated by
MUYBRIDGE.

Patent for apparatus applied for.

AUTOMATIC ELECTRO-PHOTOGRAPH.

"SALLIE GARDNER," owned by LELAND STANFORD; ridden by G. DOMM, running at a 1.40 gait over the Palo Alto track, 19th June, 1878.
The negatives of these photographs were made at intervals of twenty-seven inches of distance, and about the twenty-fifth part of a second of time; they illustrate consecutive positions assumed during a single stride of the mare. The vertical lines were twenty-seven inches apart; the horizontal lines represent elevations of four inches each.
The negatives were each exposed during the two-thousandth part of a second, and are absolutely "untouched."

Eadweard Muybridge.
The Horse in Motion, 1878.

Muybridge's obsession with motion led him to produce thousands of sequences like this one—and to invent an early form of motion pictures. The American artist Thomas Eakins also carried out important photographic locomotion studies.

dramatically altered the way photographers went about their work, especially because now all they had to carry was a camera and plates. There were even dry-emulsion tintype plates.

The birth of the dry plate led to the development of gigantic new photographic industries. Businesses like the Stanley Dry Plate Company and the Standard Dry Plate Company were established to manufacture photographic plates. Other companies arose to develop the plates, and to make prints as well, if the photographer desired; they were the beginning of the photofinishing industry.

Dry plate technology brought photograhpers one step closer to capturing motion. For the first 50 years of photography's existence, people inside and outside the medium awaited the day when cameras could capture unblurred images of people and things in motion. This feat was finally accomplished by the photographer Eadweard Muybridge. Born in England,

Muybridge came to the United States in 1850, where he became known for magnificent large prints and stereographic views of the Pacific coast, particularly in California's Yosemite region.

Muybridge's greatest photographic achievement came as the result of a bet. In 1872, the wealthy owner of a string of race horses—former governor of California and university founder Leland Stanford—wagered a friend that when a galloping horse was moving at full speed it had all four feet in the air at the same time. Since this could not be detected by the naked eye, it had always been assumed that a horse had at least one foot on the ground during full gallop. Artists had certainly painted it that way.

Stanford hired Muybridge to take pictures that would enable him to win his bet. In late 1872, Muybridge took a series of photographs of one of the owner's horses as it raced around a track. The first results were not conclusive, but they did give strong indication that, at various points, all four of the horse's feet were indeed off the ground. Stanford asked Muybridge to try again, but it was several years before he could do so. Then, in June 1877 he set up 12 cameras side by side along the straight-away portion of Stanford's track. He installed a series of threads, one to each camera, that the horse would strike breast-high, breaking them and tripping the camera shutters one after another. The images he captured proved beyond a shadow of a doubt that the horse did, at various stages of its gallop, have all four feet bunched under its stomach, well off the turf.

Muybridge's series of pictures, titled *The Horse in Motion,* was widely published. Painters, including the French military and court painter Jean Meissonier and the two most famous artists of the American West, Frederic Remington and Charles Russell, immediately changed the way they painted horses in motion. Beginning in 1884, Muybridge, photographing at the University of Pennsylvania, devoted himself to taking sequence-picture studies of people and animals on the move. Inspired by his breakthrough, inventors began developing more sophisticated equipment that would soon make freezing motion in photographs a common occurrence.

Not content with all that he had achieved, Muybridge invented a kind of giant slide projector, the *zoopraxiscope,* that could show pictures in rapid succession. He printed negatives of a sequence of pictures showing a person or animal in motion onto glass plates to get positive-image slides. These were mounted on a large cir-cular glass disk that revolved along with a slotted metal shutter disk to bring each

Making and Using a Pinhole Camera

In a high-tech age when cameras are becoming increasingly sophisticat-ed, many people are enjoying the experience of making and taking pic-tures with a pinhole cam-era, whose principles go back to the days before photography. There are even pinhole camera clubs and regularly published pinhole camera journals. Here is how to make and use a pinhole camera:

Find a can that has a tight-fitting lid. A two-pound coffee can or similar can will work fine. If the can has a plastic lid, paint the lid black on both sides, making sure that both sides are *completely* blackened. Paint the inside of the can with dull black paint or line it with black paper. All this is to make sure that no stray light enters or is reflected inside your pin-hole camera, which would ruin your pictures.

Make a pinhole in the center of the end of the can opposite the removable lid. You can make the hole in the can itself or in a sep-arate piece of thin metal, such as a two-inch square piece cut from an alu-minum frozen food or takeout food container. To make the pinhole, use a sewing needle, which you should push through up to about one-third of its length, to get the full diameter. If you make the hole in the end of the can itself, first push the needle through a cork, which will keep it from bending when you tap on it with a hammer to drive it through the metal. Use an emery board or sandpaper to remove any rough edges around the pinhole inside

the can. If you use a piece of thin aluminum, place a piece of corrugated card-board under it and cover it with a piece of cardboard such as the back of a notepaper pad before pushing the needle through (a thimble on your finger will help). Then make a hole about the size of a dime in the center of the end of the can and mount the pinhole piece over it, using *black* masking or electrical tape.

Make a shutter for your camera by cutting a flap of thick black paper to go over the pinhole. Tape it along one edge to act as a hinge and hold the oppo-site edge down with a tape tab. Fold the end of the tab over so you can lift the shutter easily. Keep the shutter closed over the pinhole except when you are taking a picture.

To load your camera, buy 4-by-5-inch or 5-by-7-inch photographic paper from a photo dealer, if available. Otherwise, buy a 10-sheet pack of 8-by-10-inch paper. Be sure to get single-weight fiber-base paper, because you will be making paper negatives to print from. Double-weight paper is too thick to print through, and RC (resin-coated) or plastic-base papers will not transmit any light. *Do not open the package in a lighted room,* or the paper will be ruined. You must be in a totally dark room illuminated only by a red 7 1/2-watt bulb, available at hardware and photo stores. Cut a piece of paper to fit inside the removable lid of your camera can. Place the paper in the lid with its emulsion (smooth, shiny)

side up. Tape all four cor-ners to hold it in place. Put the lid back on, with the shutter closed over the pinhole. Tape the lid all around its edge to prevent any possible light leaks and to ensure that it does not come off as you use the camera.

With the camera loaded, you are ready to take a picture outdoors (the light will not be strong enough indoors). You cannot hold the cam-era in your hands; it must remain perfectly steady. Use tape or a lump of modeling clay to hold the camera to a firm support, such as a porch floor or railing, the top of a patio wall, or a wooden box that you put wherever you need it. With the camera pointed at your chosen subject (one that will not move), make sure that the sun does not shine directly on the pinhole. You can shade it with your hand or a piece of cardboard if nec-essary. To make an expo-sure, lift the shutter flap to uncover the pinhole for about 30 seconds, then tape it closed again. Take the camera inside to your darkroom with the red bulb to remove the exposed paper and reload.

If you develop your own pictures, dry the paper negative and make a con-tact print from it in the normal way with the emulsion (picture) side of the paper negative toward the emulsion (shiny) side of the printing paper. Otherwise, keep all your exposed paper in a light-tight envelope until you can get a friend to develop and print your pictures for you.

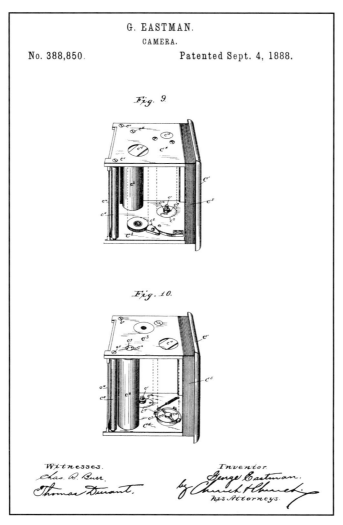

G. EASTMAN.

CAMERA.

No. 388,850.   Patented Sept. 4, 1888.

Fig. 9.

Fig. 10.

Witnesses.
Chas. R. Burr.
Thomas Durant.

Inventor
George Eastman.
by Church & Church
his Attorneys.

picture into position behind the projector lens, one after another. As the disks rotated, the audience saw a series of images on the screen. As the disks rotated faster, the images changed more rapidly until astonishingly they fused into the illusion of continuous movement. The zoopraxiscope dramatically proved that photography could not only capture movement but could reproduce it as well. Although movies, soon to be invented, used flexible film, not slides, and a completely different kind of projector, Muybridge had laid a foundation for the development of motion pictures.

The introduction of faster (more light sensitive) gelatin emulsions in the 1880s made shorter exposures possible and created a need for mechanical shutters that could open and close the lens in a fraction of a second. These developments also made it possible to hold a camera in one's hands while taking a picture, instead of mounting it on a tripod. Hand–held glass–plate

cameras were manufactured, but another major advance came when it was discovered how to coat emulsion onto a thin, transparent material called celluloid. Sheets of celluloid-base film quickly replaced glass plates. The sheets were made in the same sizes as the various standard glass plates, so the same cameras, lenses, and plate holders could be used, but the film weighed much less and did not break if it was dropped or mishandled.

Before long, many photographers realized that instead of carrying several holders loaded with individual sheets of film, it would be far more convenient if film came in continuous, flexible rolls that could be cranked through the camera to record several different negatives on a single strip. The images could be cut apart for printing after they were developed.

The man responsible for perfecting this flexible film was George Eastman. He was a pioneer in the making of dry glass plates, and in the early 1880s his factory was one of the busiest in the nation. He was a true innovator and began experimenting with a whole new system for taking pictures. He knew that his idea, if successful, would replace dry plates, but he was convinced that the flexible film he had in mind could revolutionize photography and make him an even greater fortune. After many attempts, he succeeded in perfecting a paper negative film with a gelatin emulsion. He also invented roll holders for the new film in sizes that would fit into any camera.

Eastman then went a step further. He developed a new type of hand–held camera designed to use his flexible film and to

Eastman's Brownie Camera was incredibly easy to use. To attract young users, the Brownie was named after a highly popular comic strip character and was packaged in a box that featured pictures of the well-known character.

make picture taking easier than ever before. He named his camera the Kodak and introduced it to the world in 1888. The word "Kodak" had no meaning. Always a businessman, Eastman invented a name that he thought was "catchy," was simple enough for people to remember easily, and that would be pronounced the same in almost any language.

The Kodak camera was a small box, slightly over 6 inches long, 3 1/2 inches wide, and less than 4 inches high. Inside was a roll of flexible film, enough to capture 100 pictures. (The paper-base film was replaced after the first year with Eastman's new flexible celluloid-base film.) The loaded camera cost $25. When all the pictures had been taken, the owner sent the entire camera and $10 to the Eastman Kodak factory where mounted prints were made from the negatives. The prints were then shipped back to the owner, along with the camera containing a new roll of film.

Referring to it as a "photographic notebook," George Eastman made a point of describing what he felt his camera had brought to the world. "Photography," he wrote, "is thus brought within the reach of every human being who desires to preserve a record of what he sees. Such a photographic notebook is an enduring record of many things seen only once in a lifetime and enables the fortunate possessor to go back by the light of his own fireside to scenes which would otherwise fade from memory and be lost."

To support the sales of the Kodak Camera, Eastman conducted one of the most intensive advertising campaigns that had

ever been mounted. Almost all the ads contained the slogan "You press the button, we do the rest." The response was immediate, and greater than Eastman could have imagined. Camera and other retail stores everywhere featured the Kodak. Hundreds of thousands of amateurs—ordinary people who had shied away from taking pictures because of the difficult procedures involved—eagerly paid $25 for a camera that was so easy to operate and could preserve their memories of the large and small events of their lives. That still was too expensive for many families in the 1890s, when the average laborer and shop clerk earned less than $1,000 a year. To reach them, Eastman produced smaller, less expensive Kodak models with shorter rolls of film that users could load and unload themselves. And, just after 1900 he introduced the Brownie camera, intended especially for young people, in models priced from $1 to $5. Now anyone and everyone could afford to take pictures. Total camera sales rapidly reached into the millions. The era of the snapshot had begun.

In the United States and soon in countries around the world, Kodaks were carried everywhere. The Kodak became an integral part of family gatherings, outings, and celebrations. And as the automobile became common in the early 20th century, families who found the car a new means of visiting places once considered too distant now took along a Kodak camera as naturally as they included a picnic basket and a road map. George Eastman had done much more than invent a camera. He had placed photography in the hands of millions.

George Eastman spent millions of dollars advertising his Kodak camera at the turn of the 20th century. The slogan contained in almost all of these ads became famous around the globe.

Chapter Two
Portraiture

Louis Pierson. *Countess Castiglione,* about 1860.

The French court photographer Louis Pierson took more than 400 portraits of the Countess Castiglione, considered the most beautiful woman of her time, during a 40-year collaboration. The photographs, commissioned by the countess and created under her supervision, were both self-advertisement and self-expression.

From the earliest days of photography, the taking of portraits has been by far the most common of all photographic endeavors. It would be hard to name a photographer of any merit who either did not begin by taking portraits or did not include portrait taking in his or her career.

The obvious appeal of portraits is that they provide us with a likeness of someone we know or admire. But what talented photographers have understood from the beginning is that a true portrait is not simply a record of someone's appearance, it is a visual depiction of that person's spirit and character.

In 1856, the French photographer Nadar (Gaspard Félix Tournachon) described the challenges of taking portraits with a camera. "Photography," he wrote, "is a marvelous discovery, a science that has attracted the greatest intellects, an art that excites the most astute minds.... Photographic theory can be taught in an hour, the basic technique in a day. But what cannot be taught is the feeling for light.... It is how light lies on the face that you as an artist must capture. Nor can one be taught how to grasp the personality of the sitter. To produce an intimate likeness rather than a banal portrait, the result of mere chance, you must put yourself at once in communion with the sitter, size up his thoughts and his very character."

Nineteenth-century American photographer Alice Boughton agreed with Nadar and added her own thoughts on yet another challenge of photographic portrait taking. "The painter," she explained, "usually has several sittings, sees his subject under varying conditions in different moods, has a chance, in short, to become acquainted with the personality he is to portray. The photographer, on the other hand, has one moderately short session."

Like photography itself, photographic portraiture began with the daguerreotype. Given their primitive equipment and the fact that they were learning the infant art of photography "on the job," most daguerreotypists contented themselves with producing as clear a picture as they could and on attracting as many customers as possible. Even so, many of the daguerreotypes they produced revealed more than simply what the subject of the portrait looked like.

Because of the props used in many daguerreotypes and the clothing worn by

Photographic portraiture began with the daguerreotype. From the beginning, many daguerreotypists added to the interest of their pictures by including objects that were important to their subjects.

In the early days of photography it was common practice for relatives to have pictures taken of the recently deceased before they were buried, such as this portrait of a dead preacher from 1888.

beyond just the items produced. It lets us know that at a time when it was widely believed, particularly by men, that a woman's place was in the home, the job of seamstress was one of the few wage-earning occupations open to females.

Of all those who took up photography almost immediately after the medium was introduced two Boston daguerreotypists, working between 1841 and 1862, proved to be the most accomplished portraitists of all. Their names were Albert Southworth and Josiah Hawes. Southworth had been a pharmacist before becoming fascinated with the early daguerreotypes he saw. He bought a camera from Samuel F. B. Morse and taught himself the process. Hawes, a carpenter and a part-time artist, was also self-taught. From the beginning, both partners recognized the opportunities that the newly invented field of photography presented to them. "I cannot in a letter describe all the wonders of this Apparatus," Southworth wrote of his daguerreotype camera. "Suffice it to say that I can now make a *perfect* picture in one hour's time that it would take a Painter weeks to draw." And Hawes wrote, "As I was one of the first in the business, I had the whole field before me."

Southworth and Hawes were among the most imaginative of all the daguerreotypists. Unlike their fellow pioneer photographers who posed their sitters stiffly in front of their cameras, the partners continually found ways to capture their subjects in natural postures. When one of their subjects stood by chance in a shaft of sunlight, for example, they recognized the dramatic spotlight effect and posed their subject in it. They posed some

the sitters, these early portraits often reveal much about social conditions of the times. A daguerreotype of a well-dressed seamstress posed at her sewing machine, for example, shows us that by the early 1850s the sewing machine had replaced hand stitching in much clothes production. It also provides visual evidence that the clothes-making industry had a social importance

subjects comfortably leaning against chairs or sofas and showed others in positions that suggested that they were unaware that their picture was being taken. Although they were limited to the use of sunlight coming through the studio skylights and windows, they contrasted light tones with dark so effectively that they set a standard for future photographers, even those who would have the advantage of casting light on their subjects with electrical apparatus. One of their most significant innovations was that of creating photographic "crayon portraits." Named for the charcoal and pastel style used by many artists, these pictures were distinguished by the way Southworth and Hawes created portraits by letting the head and shoulders of a subject "float" in an undefined surrounding.

Scores of the images captured by Southworth and Hawes were displayed in their elegant studio and gallery. It was but one of many similarly sumptuous galleries in the United States that, by the 1850s, captured the admiration of both American customers and foreign visitors. Here is how a French photographic journal described these establishments: "The American daguerreotypists," the journal stated, go to an enormous expense for their rooms, which are most elegantly furnished. . . . Marble, carved in columns or animated by the chisel of the sculptor, richly embroidered and costly draperies, paintings enclosed by sumptuous frames, adorn their walls. On the floor lie rich carpets where the foot falls in silence. Here are gilded cages with birds from every clime, warbling amidst exotic plants whose flowers perfume the air under the softened light of the sun.

The Challenges of Sitting for a Daguerreotype

Portraiture, like photography itself, began with the daguerreotype, and having a daguerreotype taken was a challenging experience. "It's no use going to have your portrait taken by our friend Camera unless you can sit [perfectly] still," wrote the author of one of the earliest books on photography.

In order to help their sitters hold a pose, daguerreotypists employed various props and techniques. They often had a subject lean forward with his arms on the back of a chair or couch where a second person was seated. Another technique was to place a table with a stack of books on it alongside the subject. The sitter could then hold a steady pose by placing one elbow on the books and resting his or her chin on the upraised hand.

A waist-high pedestal was also often used, to give a standing subject someplace to rest his or her hands. The most widely used device for keeping a subject still throughout the exposure was a so-called head clamp. It was a metal half-circle on a vertical rod weighted at the bottom so it would not tip over. The sitter's head could rest back against the device while his or her body concealed it from view.

For the person who wanted as pleasing a portrait as possible, sitting perfectly still was far from the only challenge. In order to get a likeness that would be acceptable to them, sitters had to assume and then maintain as natural a facial expression as possible. Since most early daguerreotype photographers were totally consumed with the technical aspects of operating the camera during the sessions, it was most often left to the subject to strike the attitude and expression he or she wanted to reveal.

Commenting on the skill required of the sitter, novelist N. P. Willis observed, "Some of us know better than others how to put on the best look. Some are handsome only when talking. Some only when the features are in repose, some have more character in the full face, some in the profile; some do the writhings of life's agonies with their hearts and wear smooth faces, some do the same work with their nostrils. A portrait-painter usually takes all these matters into account, and, with his dozen or more long sittings, has time enough to make a careful study of how the character is worked out in the physiognomy and to paint accordingly. But in daguerreotyping, the sitter has to employ this knowledge and exercise this judgement for himself."

American philosopher and author Ralph Waldo Emerson described this role of the sitter in just nine words. After having his portrait taken by a daguerreotypist who gave his full attention to the mechanics of the process, Emerson summed up his experience by stating, "The artist stands aside and lets you paint yourself."

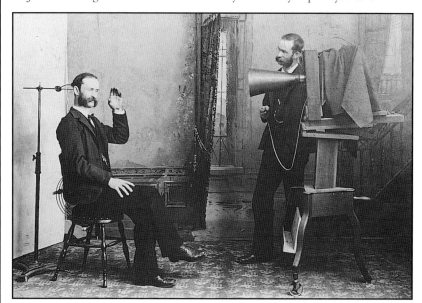

Sitting for an early daguerreotype with one's head supported by a clamp was an arduous and often painful experience. But for millions, the chance to be recorded for posterity was worth the ordeal.

Albert Southworth and Josiah Hawes. Untitled daguerreotype, about 1854.

Southworth and Hawes are considered to have been the most skilled and sensitive of all daguerreotypists, particularly in their ability to produce family portraits such as this one. As one photohistorian has noted, their greatest accomplishment was "achieving an informality and depth of character that were novel at the time."

Like many of their fellow daguerreotypists, Southworth and Hawes advertised their services widely. Many of their ads contained the statement, "We aim in our profession to please Artists, and those whose tastes for the fine arts have been cultivated and refined."

This is the American studio. Everything is here united to distract the mind of the visitor from his cares and give to his countenance an expression of calm contentment. The merchant, the physician, the lawyer, the manufacturer, even the restless politician, here forget their labors. Surrounded thus, how is it possible to hesitate at the cost of a portrait?"

It is interesting that while taking photographs is almost always an individual endeavor and partnerships in picture taking have been rare, the two most outstanding collections of early portraits were produced by photographic partnerships. Two years after Southworth and Hawes began taking their daguerreotypes, a pair of Scottish photographers joined forces and started capturing portraits by using the calotype process.

Their names were David Octavius Hill and Robert Adamson, and theirs was a true partnership, with each man responsible for specific tasks. An established portrait painter, Hill's role was to direct the taking of each portrait. He set the pose of each subject and decided which props and background would be used in each picture. Adamson worked the camera and developed and printed each photograph.

Hill and Adamson took their pictures during an era when the gulf between rich and poor in Scotland, as in many other nations, was enormously wide. It was a time when having one's portrait captured by a renowned painter or photographer was considered to be a true indication of social status. As the partners' reputation for the quality of their work grew, scores of wealthy people along with Scotland's most notable figures flocked to Hill's home, where their pictures were taken in full sunlight in front of the house. Although outside, drapes and furniture were arranged to make the picture look like an interior room. Not content

Marcelin. *Portraits of Yesteryear and Today*, 1856.

Unlike artists who could fancifully portray even their most unattractive subjects in an appealing manner, a photographer, for the most part, was limited by what his or her camera "saw." In this French cartoon, "autrefois" (yesteryear) refers to the period of portrait painting, before the advent of photography, as opposed to "aujourd'hui" (today).

with focusing solely on the rich and famous, the partners on many occasions packed all their equipment in a horsecart and hauled it off to nearby fishing villages, where they took pictures of the sailors and fishermen who inhabited the docks.

Whether their subject was a wealthy woman dressed in an elegant silk gown or a humble fisherman garbed in his working clothes, Hill's background as an artist was the greatest influence in the way they approached each portrait. Hill was arguably the first photographer to deliberately create photographs that looked like fine paintings. He brought the paintinglike contrast of shade and light to the pictures that Adamson exposed by purposely posing his sunlit subjects against dark backgrounds.

Hill was also aided by the primitive nature of the calotype itself. The paper negatives used in producing calotypes were often uneven in texture, so not all details were recorded with precision. Many of the images the partners captured looked as if they had been produced as much with a brush stroke as with a camera.

Most significant is the fact that in Hill and Adamson's finest portraits the subject seems to be engaged in something other than having a picture taken, such as reading or paying attention to something outside the frame. These "dynamic" poses give the pictures a feeling of a brief moment captured, in spite of the fact that the subject was carefully positioned to avoid any accidental movement and the exposures were on the order of 30 to 60 seconds.

Napoleon Sarony had a passion for the theater. He loved to attend performances and to be in the company of the stars of hit plays. Enchanted also with photography, he was aware that several portrait painters had built successful careers by responding to the public's appetite for likenesses of their favorite actors and actresses. In 1857 he opened a photographic studio in the heart of New York's bustling theatre district.

Sarony had a personality as colorful as the performers whose pictures he took. He dressed himself in gaudy vests, tucked his pants into high cavalry boots, and topped his outfit off with an exotic Russian hat made from curly lamb's wool. He was also a great showman. He filled his studio with exotic curiosities such as suits of armor, Egyptian mummies, and stuffed crocodiles. He used a few of them as props, but most were there simply to satisfy Sarony's desire to attract attention. It worked. Crowds peered through the windows of the studio, gazing at the objects and hoping to catch a glimpse of the actors and actresses who, in increasing numbers, came to the studio to have their pictures taken.

By the time Sarony began his portrait taking, wet plate photography had replaced the daguerreotype and the calotype as the basic photographic method. After Sarony took each of his theatrical portraits, he mounted it on a sturdy 4-by-5 1/2-inch piece of finished cardboard called a cabinet card and signed his name below the picture

Robert Adamson and David Octavius Hill. *Handyside Ritchie and John Henning*, 1850.

Hill and Adamson often added to the dramatic effect of their portraits by posing their subjects against a totally dark background, as in their portrait of two well-known English gentlemen, Handyside Ritchie and John Henning.

Napoleon Sarony. *Miss Anderson as Galatea*, about 1880.

Sarony's photograph of the actress known as Miss Anderson, in costume for a role, was typical of the flair that he brought to his theatrical portraiture.

Miss ANDERSON as GALATEA.
Copyright 1883, by Napoleon Sarony.
NEW YORK

with a flourish. He sold so many of these cabinet cards that many of the world's greatest stars and playwrights, such as Sarah Bernhardt and Oscar Wilde, always anxious for as much publicity as they could get, traveled to New York at their own expense to have Sarony take their picture.

Before Sarony's career was over, he produced some 40,000 theatrical portraits. Unlike daguerreotype and calotype portraits, which were bought almost exclusively by the subjects of these images, Sarony's pictures were purchased in great numbers by the public at large. In the process, Sarony made a great deal of money. Just as important to him, he became almost as much of a celebrity as many of those whose portraits he took.

At the same time that Napoleon Sarony was taking his celebrity portraits, Gaspard Félix Tournachon, who called himself Nadar, was taking pictures of famous people in Paris. His subjects included such celebrities as the composers Giacchino Rossini and Hector Berlioz; writers Victor Hugo, Charles Baudelaire, and George Sand; artists Honoré Daumier, Gustave Doré, Eugene Delacroix, and Jean-François Millet; the world-famous actress Sarah Bernhardt; and leading statesmen—virtually everyone of significance in art, literature, theater, politics, and intellectual endeavors.

A lithographer and accomplished caricaturist as well as a photographer, Nadar was a tireless individual. Along with his drawings, sketches, and portraits, he illustrated books and wrote novels. And he was a photographic innovator. He was the first photographer to take pictures by electric light, and produced the first photographs of the catacombs and sewers that lie underneath Paris. In 1856, he became the first person to take pictures from a balloon. But he is best remembered for the power of his portraits, images distinguished by the dramatic lighting effects he achieved by posing his subjects under a high skylight against a plain dark background.

Over the years, some portraits have been so compelling that they seem to get the very soul of the person photographed. One of the earliest of these images was Alexander

Gardner's portrait of Abraham Lincoln. A native of Scotland, Gardner moved to the United States with his family in 1856 and was soon hired by Mathew B. Brady to serve as a photographic assistant in one of his New York galleries and then as manager of Brady's Washington, D.C., establishment. When the Civil War erupted, Gardner became one of the key members of Brady's corps of photographers who so skillfully photographed almost all aspects of the conflict. His most compelling image was his Lincoln portrait, taken in 1865, just weeks before the American President was assassinated.

Abraham Lincoln was the most photographed individual of his or any previous time. One of Brady's photographs of him was used on the U.S. five-dollar bill until the year 2000, when the design of the bill was changed. Another Brady image of Lincoln, widely circulated as a carte-de-visite when he was running for President, was credited by Lincoln as being instrumental in his election. But Gardner's portrait is the most compelling of all.

In taking the picture, Gardner focused on the exhaustion and sadness expressed in Lincoln's eyes. He captured an image that went to the very soul of a man ravaged by his role as the leader of a nation at war with itself, a conflict in which more than 650,000 of his countrymen were killed. Today, more than 135 years after it was taken, Gardner's photograph remains a symbol of the tragedy of the American Civil War.

Among the early portraitists was a woman who, through the body of work she produced, is widely regarded as one of the true photographic geniuses of the 19th century. Her name was Julia Margaret Cameron and she was the wife of a distinguished English jurist and classical scholar. When their children reached adulthood, she often found herself lonely. Then her married daughter gave her a camera. The gift changed her life. She was almost 50 years old, when she took her first picture in 1863 but from that moment on photography became her great passion.

At first Cameron concentrated on taking allegorical photographs using human models to portray scenes from the Bible. Then she turned to producing photographic illustrations of well-known works of poetry. But she found her greatest joy and achieved her greatest artistry in taking portraits.

Cameron and her well-connected husband were friendly with some of the most accomplished men of their time. Their home was on the Isle of Wight, where they lived next door to the renowned poet Alfred Lord Tennyson. Among other friends were the astronomer Sir John Herschel, the

Alexander Gardner. *Portrait of Abraham Lincoln*, 1865.

Gardner's portrait of Abraham Lincoln, taken at the very end of the Civil War, revealed the anguish suffered by the man whose fate it was to have been President of a nation torn apart by a devastating war.

Julia Margaret Cameron. *Sir John Herschel,* 1869.

One of the innovations that Cameron brought to her portraiture was photographing her sitters close-up, emphasizing their faces. This technique, which she used in her portrait of British astronomer Sir John Herschel, was well ahead of its time.

Julia Margaret Cameron. *Portrait of Mary Hiller,* about 1870.

Cameron was a photographer devoted to expanding the horizons of the medium. "My aspirations," she wrote, "are to ennoble Photography and to secure for it the character and uses of High Art."

naturalist and author Charles Darwin, and poets Robert Browning and Henry Wadsworth Longfellow. Although she took hundreds of pictures of her relatives, friends, and servants, particularly the several maids who attended her and her neighbors' households, most of her time was consumed in capturing likenesses of her famous acquaintances.

In taking her portraits, Cameron often employed "improper" techniques in an effort to obtain images with a personal, intimate feeling. She sometimes adjusted her camera or used poor-quality lenses to achieve soft focus or suppress extraneous details in a picture to achieve a sense of

mood or "atmosphere" that she felt revealed the true nature of the person shown.

Above everything else Cameron was a perfectionist. She spent what seemed to her sitters like hours positioning and repositioning them and adjusting her camera until she felt they had assumed the ideal mood and expression. Her camera used full-size glass plates, which required exposures of up to five minutes. One of her neighbors, the celebrated essayist and historian Thomas Carlyle, found his one experience in front of her camera so torturous that he emphatically announced that he would never allow her to photograph him again.

Undaunted, Cameron continued to demand much of herself and her subjects. Partly it was due to her perfectionist nature. But there was a loftier reason as well. Cameron was deeply aware of both the privilege and the responsibility attached to recording the likenesses of some of the world's most important individuals. "When I have had such men before my camera," she explained, "my whole soul has endeavored to do its duty toward them in recording faithfully the greatness of the inner as well as the features of the outer man. The photograph thus taken has been almost the embodiment of a prayer."

Typical of Cameron's portraits is her photograph of famed British astronomer Sir John Herschel. As one studies the image, it becomes clear how Cameron's belief that "the eyes are the window to the soul" influenced the nature of her portraits. By using lenses that filled the picture frame with the head and shoulders of the subject, she gave photography its first true physical close-up portraits. And by capturing her subjects as they lapsed into their own thoughts or moods, she provided the first psychological close-ups as well. Cameron was able to achieve a greater intensity of connection between viewer and subject than perhaps any other 19th-century portraitist.

By the last decades of the 1880s, scores of inventions had led to revolutions in both industry and transportation. More goods were being produced around the world than ever before. People were traveling about faster and in more different ways than could ever have been imagined. It was regarded as an age of progress, a time worthy of celebration. Much of this celebration took form in a number of world's fairs and international expositions staged to honor past triumphs and to present indications of even greater accomplishments that lay ahead.

By this time also, photography had become embedded in the consciousness of people throughout the world. Camera clubs were common not only in major cities but in smaller communities as well. Photographic organizations in the United States, England, France, Germany, and other nations regularly held exhibitions, sold photographs, and awarded coveted prizes to the photographers whose work was judged most outstanding. Photographs also played a prominent role in many of the exhibits erected at the world's fairs and expositions. Some of these expositions, in fact, honored the medium itself by including a Hall of Photography.

Of all the photographs displayed at these expositions few captured visitors' attention more than images of Native Americans. By the time that these pictures were hung, the Indians had lost their bitter struggle against

As the popularity of photography increased so too did the regular appearance of major photographic exhibitions such as the annual exposition of The London Photographic Society, shown here in 1858. Commenting on the importance of such exhibitions, the London Times *claimed they were "the best attainable index of thoughts and tastes of the people who flourished during that particular year."*

Photography: International From the Beginning

Photography was born almost simultaneously in France and England, and was introduced almost immediately into the United States. It was in these locations that the various earliest forms of the medium were developed and flourished. Almost from the beginning, however, the roots of the medium were planted in other far-flung areas of the world. In a relatively short time, photography became international in scope. The following are some early examples.

In December 1839, a Belgian priest, Father Louis Compte, landed at the Brazilian port of Bahia. Father Compte was the proud owner of a daguerreotype camera and was adept at taking pictures.

News of his presence in Brazil caught the attention of Brazilian Emperor Dom Pedro II de Alcântara, who invited the priest to come to his palace in Rio de Janeiro to demonstrate the amazing procedure called photography.

Father Compte's demonstration inspired several of those in attendance to become daguerreotypists, including Florencio Valera, a resident of Uruguay who was visiting Brazil. In 1845, Valera traveled to Europe, where he bought a daguerreotype camera. When he returned to Uruguay he became instrumental in introducing photography to that nation.

Of all the Latin American countries, the daguerreotype gained the greatest popularity in Argentina.

The first photographic gallery in Argentina's capital city of Buenos Aires was opened in June 1843 by a bookseller, Gregorio Ibarra. In the next two years several foreigners also opened daguerreotype studios there, including the Americans John Bennett and John Elliot, and the Englishmen Robert Leys and Thomas Helsby. By 1850, a young Argentinean, Antonio Pozzo, had become the country's best-known daguerreotypist. Trained by both Bennett and Helsby, Pozzo photographed almost all his nation's most important figures.

As in Latin America, photography also gained an important early foothold in both New Zealand and India. In New Zealand one pioneer photographer exerted enormous influence. His name was William Meluish and he had been one of Australia's earliest daguerreotypists before opening a studio in New Zealand. Meluish not only took masterful daguerreotypes but spent much time teaching the skill to scores of aspiring photographers, including many members of his own family. In the 1860s he became equally adept both in taking cartes-de-visite and in teaching this skill as well. For the images he captured and the work of those he taught, Meluish is regarded by many as the father of New Zealand photography.

The early popularity of photography in India, particularly in Bombay, was also due in great measure to the contributions of one pioneer photographer, Hurrychind Chintamon. By the late 1850s the carte-de-visite had been introduced into India, where it became extremely popular, particularly among the wealthy people of Bombay. Chintamon was the most masterful and most successful of the early Indian photographers who captured carte-de visite images of literary, political, and business figures. Chintamon's most famous carte was a portrait of the Maharaja of Baroda. Thousands of these images were distributed throughout India. Countless others were sent to places as far away as China, where they may well have been the first photographs many people there had ever encountered.

the imposing white civilization, had been stripped of their lands, and had been forcibly moved onto United States government reservations. Aware that people everywhere were fascinated by the rich and ancient cultures of the Indians, by their dress and customs, and by the stories of the heroic deeds they had performed, promoters paid many Native Americans to leave their reservations temporarily and appear and be photographed at the expositions.

One of the scores of photographers who took advantage of this opportunity was Nebraska photographer Frank Rinehart. As the official photographer of the Trans-Mississippi International Exposition of 1898, Rinehart took scores of Native American portraits. He was an accomplished photographer, with a flair for the dramatic. But he was also a sensitive man, well aware of the tragic fate the Indians had suffered. His image of a young Indian chief dressed in a war bonnet and other symbols of his rank is typical of the insight he brought to all his portraits. Reflected in the chief's expression is the fierce pride of the Native Americans. But etched in his face also is the sadness of a people who had lost so much.

Frank Rinehart succeeded in preserving images of people whose ways of life had forever changed. Two other photographers, August Sander and Doris Ulmann, undertook lengthy projects in which they sought, through portraits, to reveal specific classes of people and the type of work they did.

Sander and Ulmann lived worlds apart. Sander, a German, was a person of modest means from a family of coal miners. Ulmann was a very wealthy American. Self-taught in photography, Sander began his project in 1911 when he was 35 years old. He titled it *Man of the Twentieth Century.* He began by making a list of the various occupational types he wished to portray. He decided to take most of his photographs in his native Westerwald region because he knew it so well. "These people whose way of life I had known from my youth," he wrote, "appealed to me because of their closeness to nature." Each day he rode his bicycle to a different area of the region, where he captured portraits of tradesmen, laborers, and countless other types. Because Sander was known to them, his subjects posed willingly for his camera. The trust they had both in his abilities and in the nature of his project resulted in the naturalness of each of the images he captured.

Sander's plan was to capture some 600 portraits of his countrymen. But because he had the misfortune to be photographing as the German Nazi regime came into power, he was able to capture far fewer images. In 1929 he produced a book featuring many of the photographs he had already taken. The Nazis eventually banned the book, raided his studio, and destroyed many pictures, because they felt that Sander's honest pictures depicted people not representative of the master race they wished to create. Determined to save as much of his work as possible, Sander hid his negatives in the countryside. After the Nazis were defeated in World War II, the negatives that

had survived were reclaimed, newly printed, and widely distributed. Today they are recognized as a masterful depiction of a particular people at a specific time in history.

Much of August Sander's photographic genius lay in his ability to avoid stereotyping the people he photographed. His pictures reveal the individuality of his subjects as well as their social roles. The same can be said of many of the portraits taken by Doris Ulmann.

Ulmann learned photography by attending courses taught by the master photographic teacher Clarence White, one of the

Frank Rinehart. Portrait of an Indian chief, about 1880.

Each article of clothing and ceremonial equipment with which a Native American chief adorned himself had tribal or cultural significance. Whenever they could, portraitists of the Native Americans, like Rinehart, posed their subjects attired in authentic costume.

August Sander. Coal delivery man, about 1915.

Sander's Man of the Twentieth Century *photographic project included this image of a man whose job it was to deliver coal. Sander defined the purpose of his project by stating, "Let me speak the truth in all honesty about our age and the people of our age."*

leaders of the art photography movement called pictorialism (see Chapter 4). During the first decade of the 1900s, she concentrated on taking portraits of the scores of rich and famous men and women who traveled in the same social circles as she did. Eventually, however, she became bored with this work.

She decided to undertake a personal project that would result in portraits of a very different type of people. She chose as her subjects the men, women, and children whose families had, for generations, been living in the remote Appalachian region of the United States. At a time when an enormous tide of immigration had recently changed the face of the United States, she became determined to preserve the faces of

what she and many others regarded as American types.

Attended by a servant, driven by a chauffeur, and attired in a spotless white dress and gloves, Ulmann traveled throughout the mountains and valleys of Appalachia carrying out her project. Unlike August Sander, she was completely unknown to those whose portraits she took. Her lifestyle was as different from theirs as could be imagined. These were simple, hard-working people whose families for generations had experienced none of the luxuries and few of the conveniences of life. Yet she had a marvelous ability to put each of those she photographed at ease.

Although her training in pictorialism often is evident in the style of her portraits, they go beyond being illustrations or art studies. They not only reveal the character of her subjects but include many of the objects that were a vital part of their everyday lives. The images she captured became important not only to people interested in photography but to sociologists and historians as well. Her portrait of an Appalachian woman, for example, reveals the distinctive head covering that women in that region had worn for generations. The picture thus includes evidence of a sustained, unchanging cultural element. By producing such a vital depiction, Doris Ulmann, like August Sander, gave a whole new meaning to what portraiture could achieve.

Another woman photographer, Consuelo Kanaga, devoted much of her portrait work to African Americans. "I love to photograph black people," Kanaga stated, "to try to capture the strength and dignity I so

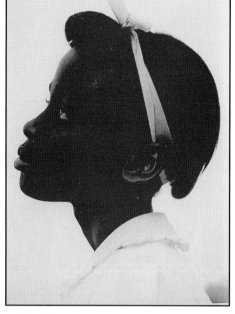

Consuelo Kanaga. *Young Girl in Profile,* 1948.

Kanaga was a deeply spiritual person. She believed that by portraying the inner beauty of her subjects she was performing a religious exercise.

often find in their faces." Kanaga was only 21 when, in 1915, she became one of the first female news photographers, working first for the *San Francisco Chronicle* and later for the *San Francisco Daily News.* The news photographs she took and the photo essays she created for these and other publications in the 1920s through the 1940s went beyond demonstrating her skill with a camera. They revealed the deep compassion she felt for all those she photographed, particularly those living in poverty or affected by such injustices as racial prejudice.

Kanaga's greatest photographic passion, however, was that of taking portraits. And it was through portraiture that she captured many of her most vital images. She was a meticulous worker who spent long hours in the darkroom. "I found," she wrote late in her life, "that my portraits really stand on their own because I put a lot into them and wanted them to be beautiful. I had to make fifty prints to get one that I liked, so that's why I never did get rich."

Kanaga's compassion for her subjects and her appreciation of the beauty of black facial features can be seen in portraits such as *Young Girl in Profile* and *Frances with a Flower.* In *Young Girl in Profile,* Kanaga achieved the dramatic effect she sought by contrasting the dark skin and hair of her subject with the whiteness of her blouse and hair ribbon. She enhanced the contrast by having light fall upon the girl's ear and lower lip. Her ability to contrast deep shades of black with splashes of brilliant whites is evident also in *Frances with a Flower.* Here the white of the flower provides the contrast. By taking this portrait

close-up, Kanaga was able to emphasize the texture of the girl's black skin which she admired so much.

The work of outstanding studio portraitists in the 19th and early 20th centuries paved the way for Consuelo Kanaga and the many others who, in modern times, have continued to make portraiture a vital form of photography. Modern formal portrait photographers have recognized that the basic elements that go into capturing an outstanding portrait—pose, facial expression, lighting, and props—have remained virtually the same as in earlier days. Most important, they are aware that masterful portraits are those that depict much more than a simple likeness of the subject.

There is another link with the past as well. Just as early portrait photographers such as Mathew Brady and Napoleon Sarony built careers on the public's appetite for pictures of the well known, many modern photographers have attained significant success by recording the likenesses of famous men and women.

Among these photographers was the Canadian Yousuf Karsh. In 1924, when he was 15 years old, Karsh fled Turkish brutality in his native Armenia (then part of Turkey). He went to live with an uncle who had a photographic studio in the Canadian province of Quebec. When the uncle discovered that Yousuf had a talent for photography, he arranged for his nephew to be apprenticed to the successful Boston portrait photographer John Garo.

Karsh remained with Garo for three years, learning the techniques that would eventually distinguish his work. Among

Consuelo Kanaga. *Frances with a Flower,* 1948.

Yousuf Karsh. *Winston Churchill, 1941.*

Karsh spent more than 50 years photographing the most famous people in the world, including Prime Minister Winston Churchill of Britain. The acclaim he received was so widespread that he became as famous as the celebrities whose portraits he took.

these techniques was an emphasis on strong lighting, making visible the smallest characteristic details of the face, which would become his hallmark. During his apprenticeship Karsh also discovered that the most effective portraits he took were those in which he relied on his subjects' poses and facial expressions rather than on props or elaborate settings. And he discovered something else: What he enjoyed most was meeting and photographing famous people.

When his apprenticeship was over, he chose to establish himself as a photographer in Ottawa, Canada. His fascination with famous people was a key factor in his decision. Not only had he fallen in love with Canada, but as he later expressed it, "It was the best choice I could have made, for Canada's capital city was soon to become one of the important crossroads of the world, a frequent meeting place for the giants of the earth."

For more than the next 50 years, Karsh, using Ottawa as his base, traveled the world taking portraits with his distinctive lighting style of many of the best-known people of the mid 20th century. His subjects included British Prime Minister Winston Churchill, United States Presidents Franklin D. Roosevelt, Harry S. Truman, and Dwight D. Eisenhower, first lady Eleanor Roosevelt, authors Ernest Hemingway and H. G. Wells, architect Frank Lloyd Wright, and singer Paul Robeson. Many of those who sat for his camera regarded their Karsh portrait as the most revealing that had ever been taken of them. As photohistorian Peter Pollock observed, "Yousuf Karsh, in his powerful portraits, transforms the human face into legend."

Some contemporaries of Karsh also became masters of portraiture in the mid 20th century, a period that saw the growth of much photographic innovation. Portraits by the American Arnold Newman are marked by dramatic lighting and bold, graphic composition. He too trained his camera mainly on well-known individuals, but he photographed them in their own environments, surrounded by the objects of their professions or the tools of their trades, rather than in the studio. Latvian-born Phillipe Halsman came to the United States in 1940, after 20 years as a photographer in Paris. He also photographed celebrities, with a psychologically penetrating and graphically dramatic style. He sometimes created fantasy-image portraits, such as a picture of Salvador Dali in which everything is suspended in midair, as in one of Dali's surrealist paintings. Halsman's delight in the spontaneous and unexpected led him to persuade many of his subjects to participate in a moment of play at the end of a portrait session. The amusing, and often revealing, results are collected in a book titled *Jumpbook,* which consists entirely of pictures of otherwise distinguished people jumping into the air.

Today we live in a world where we are surrounded by portraits. Photographs of famous men and women appear on many of the postage stamps we use. Family portraits adorn many of the Christmas cards we receive. An important part of every school year for parents and children alike is the annual school portrait. In most societies no wedding is considered complete without the official wedding portraits. The pages of the newspapers and magazines we read are filled with the pictures of the famous and the lesser known. Through these portraits in print, we are able to discover much about the diversity of populations and the differences in social classes.

Portraits have become so important that they are used as a means of proving that we are who we claim to be. Driver's licenses, passports, and many credit cards are not considered valid unless they contain a photographic image of the bearer.

Despite the many distinct areas of photography that have emerged since its invention—such as photojournalism, social documentary, scientific and technical photography, advertising, fashion, and commercial illustration—many professional photographers still concentrate on taking portraits. Almost every sizable city or town has at least one portrait studio. Some, like

Boston's generations-old Bachrach studio, have earned proud reputations for the quality of their work. Still, the vast majority of portraits are taken by nonprofessionals.

Most of us, without realizing it, are in fact amateur portraitists. Whenever we capture a likeness of a relative or friend, whether with a highly sophisticated camera or a point-and-shoot, disposable model, we are in reality taking a portrait. The family albums that we cherish and the informal, candid pictures of relatives and friends that adorn our refrigerator doors and sit on our mantelpieces and tables are perhaps the best reminders of all, not only of photography's popularity but of how portraiture in particular has come to play such an important role in our lives.

Walker Evans. *Penny Picture Display, Savannah,* 1936.

Portraiture has, from the beginning, been the most common form of photography. A sign outside a photographer's studio shows faces of all ages.

Chapter Three
The World Around Us

From the time that photography was first introduced, one of its greatest appeals was its potential for bringing viewers authentic scenes of places that few people would ever be able to visit in person. Some daguerreotypists, aware of this interest, had captured landscape images. But the quality and scope of their pictures was limited by the difficulty of truly mastering the process, the small size of the images (usually 3 1/4 by 4 1/4 inches), and particularly the one-of-a-kind nature of daguerreotypes. By the late 1850s, however, even though photography had been in existence for less than 20 years, things had changed dramatically. Thanks to the development of the wet plate process, which required less exposure time than the daguerreotype or calotype, clear images of nature could now be captured far more easily.

Most of the photographers, both amateur and professional, who began to train their cameras on the land chose to take their pictures close to home. Many concentrated on the unique characteristics of the terrain that surrounded them. By the 1860s, it became commonplace for almost all photographers, even those who made their living taking portraits, to spend at least some time taking pictures of the landscape in their locale.

At the same time, there were other photographers who recognized the public's growing desire for views of exotic and far-off places. They began to travel thousands of miles in order to meet this demand. One of the distant areas that became a favorite target of these photographers was the Near East. People around the globe had always been fascinated with this region, which had given birth to some of the world's earliest civilizations. Of particular interest were the fabled pyramids and other ancient monuments and temples that had been erected thousands of years ago, structures that had long been ranked among the wonders of the world. Stereograph companies found they could sell stereo cards of Egypt and the Holy Land in enormous numbers. Individual photographers discovered that there was real profit to be made in establishing their own companies, set up to sell the views they took to Near East tourists and armchair travelers around the world.

The interest in exotic lands also led to the publication of some of the world's first photographically illustrated books. The

Photographer unknown.
Photographing Avalon Bay,
California, 1906.

As cameras and other photographic equipment improved, photographers increasingly took pictures of the world around them. Soon many were plying their trade in even the most distant places.

Henri Béchard. *Ascending the Great Pyramid,* 1878.

The pictures taken by the early photographers of the Near East helped shrink the world. "Every day now lessens the distance between the traveled and the untraveled man," reported the British *Journal of the Photographic Society in 1857.*

means of reproducing photographs on a printed page had not yet been invented, but publishers began to enhance the appeal of their books about travel and foreign places by pasting photographs onto their pages. Illustrators also copied pictures taken in distant places or used them as reference to make engravings, which had long been the basic form of book and magazine illustrations. One of the first significant publishers of photo-illustrated books was Louis Desiré Blanquart-Evrard. His 1852 publication of a volume featuring pictures that the masterful French photographer Maxime Du Camp had taken in Egypt, Palestine, and Syria was highly successful.

Between the late 1850s and 1880s, scores of photographers trained their cameras on the Near East. The photographic

expeditions they mounted resembled military campaigns. Many employed teams of porters to carry the dozens of huge crates that contained their cameras, heavy glass plates, developing chemicals, and other equipment. To get the pictures they sought, these photographers traveled enormous distances by camel, mule, and boat. Often they were forced to cross desert sands in searing heat. Yet they produced tens of thousands of photographs. In the process, they established themselves as pioneers of landscape photography.

Two of the most talented of these early cameramen were the Englishman Francis Frith and the Frenchman Félix Bonfils. Between 1856 and 1860, Frith made three expeditions to the Near East. While photographing there he used three different types of cameras. One of them was a stereograph camera. Another used 8-by-10-inch glass plates. The third was an enormous mahogany camera which took mammoth images 16 by 20 inches in size. Frith often photographed the same scene with all three cameras. He did this so that he could sell as many pictures in as many different forms as possible.

Frith's adventures on his picture-taking journeys were indicative of the types of challenges almost all the early photographers encountered in the ancient lands. He was captured by bandits in the Sinai Desert. Twice he was shipwrecked on the little steamboat that carried him up and down the Nile River. But by the time he had completed his three photographic journeys to the Holy Land area, he had taken enough appealing images to assure the success of his own photographic company.

Like Frith, Félix Bonfils's motive for taking photographs of the Near East was to produce an inventory of pictures to be sold throughout the world. Actually, many of the photographs attributed to Bonfils were undoubtedly taken by his wife Marie. An accomplished photographer in her own right, Marie accompanied her husband on many of his photographic journeys.

The Bonfilses began photographing in the Near East in the early 1860s. By 1871 they had taken so many pictures there that their company boasted a stock of 15,000 prints and 9,000 stereographic views. Unlike many of their counterparts whose only goal was to produce images that they felt would sell briskly, the Bonfilses paid serious attention to the artistic quality of their photographs as well. Their focus on composition and contrast can be seen throughout the body of work they produced.

While most of the early photographers of the Near East financed their own photographic ventures, landscape photography on a grand scale was introduced in the United States by photographers employed by the federal government. These cameramen were hired to accompany the surveying expeditions of the vast unsettled territories of the American West that took place in the late 1860s and early 1870s.

One of the first of these survey photographers was Carleton E. Watkins. He had actually taken scores of photographs of the spectacular landscape of northern California's Yosemite Valley before the initial government expeditions were launched. Through images he captured on his own, such as that of the mountain called El Capitan, and those he took for the government,

Francis Frith. *Colossus of Ramses II at Abu Simbel, Nubia,* about 1862.

Frith's photograph of this ancient colossal figure was taken at Abu Simbel in Egypt. Looking back on the challenges he faced taking pictures of the landscapes and antiquities of the East, Frith wrote, "When I reflect on the circumstances under which the photographs were taken, I marvel greatly that they turned out so well."

Félix Bonfils. *Pyramid of Cheops,* about 1870.

Marie and Félix Bonfils were among the most successful of all the early photographers of the Near East. They published catalogues of their images and sold their pictures through dealers in the larger cities of Europe and America.

Carleton Watkins. *El Capitan,*
about 1866.

*In taking his pictures of the
American West, Watkins often
focused on magnificent scenery
reflected in a lake in the foreground
of his image. It was a technique
quickly adopted by many other
landscape photographers.*

Watkins revealed himself as a photographer
in love with nature. His images present us
with the pure and sublime qualities of a
landscape that was soon to be encroached
upon by humans.

Timothy O'Sullivan was another specially gifted survey photographer. He had
earned much acclaim for the scores of
images he had captured as a member of
Mathew Brady's corps of Civil War photographers. His experience in taking pictures under the most difficult field conditions served him well in coping with the
challenges he faced in the rugged terrain of
the western lands. The survey photographs
he took are marked not only by his talent
at photographing broad landscapes, but also
by his ability to capture details of the virgin
territory such as the plant life and natural
rock formations that he encountered.

Another survey cameraman, John Hillers,
adopted a special approach. Hillers, the official photographer for an 1871 government
expedition down the Colorado River, was
awestruck by the enormity of the landscape
of that region. In order to convey this
through his photographs he often posed a
lone figure against a majestic backdrop.

Some of the most compelling of all the
survey photographs were those taken by
William Henry Jackson. In 1866, Jackson
left Vermont, where he had been a photographer's apprentice, and traveled west as a
bullwhacker driving an ox team. In 1869,
he met Dr. Frank F. V. Hayden, the leader of
an upcoming survey, who invited Jackson
to join the expedition as its cameraman.
From that 1870 undertaking until 1879,
Jackson served as official photographer for
eight geological surveys. He was the first

cameraman to record the amazing features of the Yellowstone area. The pictures that he took in that region were so spectacular that they helped convince Congress to make Yellowstone the nation's first national park.

The difficulties that O'Sullivan and the other survey photographers encountered in capturing their images were equal to those faced by the early photographers in the Near East and other parts of the world. The lands through which the western survey expeditions traveled were places dominated by high, often dangerous mountains and deep valleys. Rapidly flowing rivers ran throughout the region. The photographers hauled their large cameras and heavy glass plates up mountains and along rivers knowing that they had to develop each image they captured on the spot. Almost every one of these cameramen experienced a particular kind of photographic tragedy at least once. They would lug their equipment thousands of feet up a mountain and then develop the negatives in the special darkroom tent they also had to haul during the wet plate period. On the way down the mountain there was always the danger that the mule or horse carrying the developed glass plates might stumble or even fall off the side of the mountain, shattering the

Timothy O'Sullivan. Photographer's wagon, about 1867.

This horse-drawn wagon was used by a United States government photographic survey team as it made its way through the vast desert territory of the American West. Traveling huge distances with heavy equipment and coping with desert heat were but two of the many hardships these photographers endured as they compiled their photographic record.

William Henry Jackson. *Mammoth Hot Springs, Yellowstone, Wyoming,* 1871.

The government survey photographers captured the unusual terrain they encountered as they made their way west. These natural hot springs were made even more spectacular by their tiered rock formation. Artist Thomas Moran, shown climbing the rocks, also documented the western landscape.

plates. A day's or even a week's arduous work could be lost in an instant. But the results were well worth their efforts.

The photographs that these cameramen took not only captured the majesty of unspoiled regions that few white people had ever encountered, but set a photographic standard for all landscape photographers who would follow. There were other results as well. Once the surveys were concluded, prints of the photographs were brought to Washington, D.C., where they were put on display at several government institutions.

Eventually the survey photographs were catalogued and housed in various archives such as the Library of Congress, the National Archives, and the Smithsonian Institution. Over the years, thousands of private citizens from around the world have purchased prints of these pioneering landscape images from these archives at inexpensive prices. Publishers have included selections of these photographs in scores of books.

At the same time that the survey photographers were taking their pictures, another group of cameramen was also operating in the American West. These were photographers hired by the railroad companies to document the building of the western railway lines. One of the earliest of

these cameramen was William Henry Jackson, who before becoming a premier survey photographer had documented the construction of the Union Pacific Railroad. The pictures that the railroad photographers took recorded not only the progress of the railroad construction, but the grandeur of the surroundings in which the building adventure was taking place.

Among the most dramatic of the images captured by the railroad photographers were those taken by Andrew J. Russell. As the official photographer first for the Central Pacific Railroad and later for the Union Pacific Railroad, Russell, like Timothy O'Sullivan, had honed his skills as a Civil War cameraman. His railroad pictures included views of the building crews as they tunneled through deep mountains, laid track over vast areas of open land, and

carried out the scores of other tasks related to the construction enterprise. His most spectacular photographs were those he took of the enormous bridges and trestles they built to carry the tracks and trains across the many rivers and gorges along the railway route. It was through these photographs in particular that Russell most effectively conveyed the sense of awe he felt as he confronted both the railway workers' accomplishments and the land upon which their achievements took place.

The landscape and expedition photographers of the 1850s through the 1880s were employed primarily to make objective records of what they saw. Their images often have great beauty precisely because of the straightforward manner in which they present the variety and grandeur of nature. In the 1890s, a new kind of nature

Andrew J. Russell. Train on railroad bridge, 1868.

Russell captured this image of a newly constructed bridge in Utah's towering Weber Canyon. The heavy locomotives and railway cars had been rolled on to the bridge to test the strength of the new structure.

The Mammoth Camera

During most of the 19th century, making enlargements of pictures was not practical. Until the mid 1880s, all printing papers had to be exposed by sunlight, in contact with the negative, which remained the preferred way of printing into the 20th century. There were a few enlargers that used mirrors or were fitted to openings in opaque window shutters to direct sunlight through the negative, but they were so large, slow, and difficult to operate that they were not widely used. Whatever size print he wanted, a photographer had to use a plate or film that size in the camera. Many of the photog-

raphers of the American West, for example, used huge cameras capable of handling glass plates as large as 11 by 14 inches or even 16 by 20 inches.

The largest camera ever built was the one created especially for an American photographer, George R. Lawrence. He was hired by the Chicago and Alton Railroad Company to make highly detailed photographs of their newly built luxury train. Appropriately named "The Mammoth," the camera weighed 1,400 pounds when loaded with its 500-pound glass plate negative and was 20 feet long with its bellows extended for focusing. It took as many as 15 men to operate the device; expo-

sures in bright sunlight were about 2 1/2 minutes long.

The 4 1/2-by-8-foot picture of the train that the camera took was so unique that it was awarded the Grand Prize of the World at the Paris Exposition of 1900. The camera was used on a few other occasions to photograph large interiors, one of which was at the huge Chicago meatpacking headquarters of Swift and Company. Flash powder, a forerunner of flashbulbs, was used for illumination. Three hundred charges of the powder, hidden around the large area, were ignited simultaneously. However, The Mammoth proved to be far too big, cumbersome, and difficult to operate and was quickly retired from use.

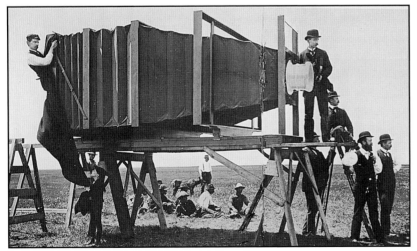

The Mammoth camera was one of the largest photographic devices ever made. Although too large to be practical, it impressed all who saw it.

photographer emerged alongside those who practiced the documentary approach. These new photographers wanted to interpret the beauty of nature, not simply to record or document it. Their concern was with pictorial beauty rather than literal accuracy, and they tended to look on landscape scenes much as painters did. They appeared first in Europe, where the Scotsman James Craig Annan was representative of the scores of photographers who found their subject matter in the landscapes of the British Isles and the countries of Europe.

Annan's father, Thomas, was a well-known photographer, and the son James was introduced to the medium at a very early age. He spent his formative years working in his father's studio. When he went out on his own as a photographer, James Annan found his greatest satisfaction photographing out-of-doors. The images he produced differed from those of many landscapists. Rather than giving viewers a general impression of an area, his pictures provided viewers with a glimpse of a port or a farmyard or a castle-dominated hillside much in the same manner as a traveler would first encounter them. Among his most popular photographs was the image titled *Stirling Castle*. This picture reveals Annan's ability to create an instant impression of a scene. The light shining on the white horse captures our immediate attention. It is only after looking more closely at the image that we begin to observe the details of the farmyard and the presence of the castle looming atop the cliffs. Annan's approach proved highly successful. His photographs were widely exhibited throughout Europe in the 1890s and the

James Craig Annan. *Stirling Castle*, 1903.

Annan brought a painter's eye to his landscape photographs. The contrast between the dark shadows and the white horse, along with the sharp planes of the buildings stretching from foreground to background, give this photograph a rare three-dimensional effect.

first decades of the 1900s and were reproduced in photography art publications in the United States.

Although Annan came to reject the subjective and interpretive extremes of pictorial photography, that approach dominated much of landscape and nature photography around the globe through the 1920s. Then, the "straight" approach, which used objective seeing and straightforward technique to create images of the beauty of nature, reappeared and gained great strength of artistic expression.

In 1930, a young Californian named Ansel Adams gave up his ambition of becoming a concert pianist in favor of a new pursuit. A passionate nature-lover, as early as 1916 he had begun taking what would eventually be thousands of pictures of the natural scenes that he encountered in his native California, greatly influenced by the pictorial style. But by the late 1920s he had come to feel the need to make more artistically honest and powerful images, and when he finally made the decision to pursue

photography rather than music as a career, he was dedicated to the straight approach. He captured both landscapes on the grandest scale and details of small nat-ural objects. He was happiest photograping such subjects as rocky deserts, mist-shrouded mountains, trees, and other plants, and was particularly sensitive to the play of sunlight and moonlight on these subjects. His pictures, from small prints to giant photomurals of the grandeur of the American West and the national parks of the United States, became world famous long before his death in 1984.

Adams's training as a pianist had a great bearing on his long photographic career. He appreciated the need to have excellent technique and to make an impressive presentation. This was reflected in his statement, "The negative is the score, the print is the performance." His acknowledged masterpieces are large-scale images with a rich tonal range from deep textured blacks to creamy whites that emphasize the majesty and grandeur of nature—a kind of

Ansel Adams. *Dunes, Oceano, California,* about 1963.

Adams approached his work with a deeply felt reverence for the unspoiled landscape he photographed. As one critic observed, "Adams photographs seem to demonstrate that our world is what we would wish it was—a place with room in it for new beginnings."

photographic grand opera of which he was the impresario.

Ansel Adams was one of the medium's most articulate spokesmen. Rarely has any photographer's motivations for capturing images been expressed as eloquently as Adams's when he wrote, "I believe man must be free, both in spirit and society, that he must build strength into himself, affirming the enormous beauty of the world and acquiring confidence to see and to express his vision. And I believe in photography as one means of expressing this affirmation, and achieving an ultimate happiness and faith."

The introduction first of the wet plate and then the dry plate, which made landscape photography on a grand scale a reality also made it possible for photographers to capture architectural images more effectively than ever before. Architectural photography is actually as old as the medium itself. In his book *The Pencil of Nature,* published in 1844–46, William Henry Fox Talbot discussed many of the potential applications of photography. Pictures of architecture, monuments, and similar

structures would be of great value in teaching architects, designers, and historians, he pointed out, as well as their obvious use for reference. In addition, they would bring some of the wonders of ancient and modern building to a much wider, nonprofessional audience who would both enjoy and benefit from them. The book was illustrated with calotypes, some of which showed exactly these kinds of subjects.

Hill and Adamson, in addition to their portraits, made many calotype studies in the mid 1840s of buildings, monuments, and ruins throughout Scotland. In the late 1850s, two Englishmen, Dr. John McCosh and Captain Linnaeus Tripe, produced images of buildings and structures in India using the calotype. And the photographs taken in the Near East by Francis Frith, Félix Bonfils, and others were often as important for their depictions of ancient monuments, temples, forts, and palaces as they were for their portrayals of the surrounding landscape.

Other major architectural photographic projects in the mid 19th century included recording the rehabilitation of French cathedrals that had fallen into disrepair in the preceding 200 years. By the last decades of the century, professional and amateur photographers throughout the world were training their cameras on monumental and historic structures. This was particularly true in Europe, where one did not have to travel far to encounter such buildings. Almost every city, and indeed many towns, contained towering cathedrals, churches, and cloisters, which were among the most favored of all architectural subjects.

Arguably, the most outstanding of all the architectural photographers was the Englishman Frederick Henry Evans. As a young man he was a successful bookseller. He turned to photography because he felt that the medium, above all others, presented him the opportunity to express the beauty he found in so many man-made structures. Most of all, he was taken with the glory of the cathedrals that he continually encountered in England and on the European continent.

Frederick Evans brought a whole new element to architectural photography. Whereas most of his counterparts focused on the magnificence of the exteriors of the cathedrals as they rose into the sky, Evans found the greatest beauty deep inside the structures. He took his camera down to the cellars of the cathedrals and into narrow side aisles as well as into the huge main chambers, where he photographed the massive pillars, the soaring flights of stairs, and the patches of sunlight playing upon ancient stone floors.

Evans's photograph *The Sea of Steps— Wells Cathedral* is particularly compelling. In describing the image he stated, "The beautiful curve of the steps on the right is for all the world like the surge of a great wave.... It is one of the most imaginative lines it has been my good fortune to try and depict."

In taking their pictures, Evans and the other architectural photographers made a contribution beyond that of producing beautiful images. The photographs inspired travelers to visit the structures that were depicted. Architects everywhere studied the images for the examples of superior design they revealed. Many of these photographs are still used for the same purpose.

The photographs of natural wonders and man-made marvels that were produced in ever-increasing numbers went a long way toward satisfying the public's desire for pictures of places and things they would probably never see in person. Yet there was another category of photographs that people around the world were just as eager to view. These were images of people from far-off lands, their ethnic cultures, and their ways of life.

In response, scores of photographers from different nations undertook photographic projects, some enormous in scope, designed to fill this need. Four photographers in particular, the Russian cameraman

Frederick Evans. *The Sea of Steps—Wells Cathedral*, 1903.

Evans was motivated by his belief in the power of photography to preserve a record of the great architecture of the world. "Without such records," he wrote, "it will be impossible for succeeding generations to form any proper idea of [these] wonders."

Sergei Mikhailovich Prokudin-Gorskii. Russian peasants, about 1915.

This photograph of a Russian family outside their simple home was typical of the thousands of images Prokudin-Gorskii captured of a land and people practically unknown to the outside world. His endeavor remains one the most ambitious individual photographic projects.

Sergei Mikhailovich Prokudin-Gorskii, the Swedish photographers Eric and Edith Matson, and the American Edward S. Curtis, serve as prime examples.

Sergei Mikhailovich Prokudin-Gorskii, a native of St. Petersburg, Russia, was descended from one of the oldest and noblest families in his province. He studied both science and art, but what he really wanted to be was a violinist. A laboratory accident at school, however, left him with a badly injured hand and he turned his attention to chemistry.

After pursuing advanced studies and serving as a chemistry instructor, Prokudin-Gorskii began to undertake various scientific experiments. He made several breakthroughs in various areas, but the most important of all was his development of an early form of color-sensitive photographic plates. By

1905 he had begun to take color pictures that could then be turned into slides and projected upon a screen.

Prokudin-Gorskii became so fascinated with photography that he decided to make it his life's work. Aside from his passion for the medium, he had several other motivations for doing so. He was in love with the traditions and history of his country. He was deeply disturbed that Russian photographers had lagged so far behind their counterparts in other nations. He was also a great supporter of Russia's leader Tsar Nicholas II and felt that, through a special photographic project he had in mind, he could help the tsar become known as the leader who had led his people to an understanding of their traditions and heritage.

The project that Prokudin-Gorskii wished to pursue was extraordinarily ambitious. His plan was to photograph all of the Russian Empire—its natural beauties, its buildings, and most important, its diverse people. He knew that such an undertaking was one that no single person could afford. It would require special equipment and travel by railroad, ship, and wagon over extremely long distances. Such a project could be made possible only by the financial and political support of the tsar.

Prokudin-Gorskii used all the considerable influence he had with various Russian officials to obtain a meeting with those who could pave the way for a presentation of his project to the tsar. Once he succeeded in arranging such a meeting, he spent weeks taking photographs that would best illustrate what he wanted to accomplish. When the high Russian officials saw the photographs, they arranged a demonstration to the tsar and the royal family. Tsar

Nicholas, in turn, was so impressed with the images that he agreed to finance the photographic project, to supply whatever transportation Prokudin-Gorskii required during his photographic journeys, and to give him official papers assuring the cooperation of all those he met along the way.

From 1909 to 1917, Prokudin-Gorskii traveled the length and breadth of Russia photographing the peasants and villagers who lived in farms, hamlets, and towns throughout the nation. He also captured images of valleys, rivers, and churches in each region where he stopped. He compiled an extraordinary photographic record, particularly of people few outsiders had ever seen. His work was brought to a halt in 1917 when World War I broke out and Tsar Nicholas was overthrown in what became known as the Russian Revolution. Forced to flee his beloved country, Prokudin-Gorskii lived out the rest of his life in exile in Norway, England, and France.

Eric Matson was eight years old when, in 1896, he and his parents, along with several other families, moved from Sweden to Palestine, where they joined a community of Americans in what became known as the American Colony. The Colony's purpose was to supply aid to the sick and needy of Jerusalem and surrounding areas. Among its other activities was one that came to change the lives of Eric Matson and the woman who became his wife. In 1898 the German Kaiser, Wilhelm II, visited Palestine. The American Colony hastily organized a photographic department to record the historic visit. The photographs that were produced proved to be of such interest to German officials and to others who viewed them that the Colony decided to make the photographic department a permanent part of its operations, with its main purpose that of satisfying the needs of tourists anxious to bring back pictures of the people and places of the region.

G. Eric Matson. Shepherd with his flock, about 1935.

Matson took this picture at a spring located about seven miles outside of the ancient city of Jerusalem. He used the image as the first in a series he created illustrating the 23rd Psalm ("The Lord is my shepherd…")

Edward Curtis. Kutenai duck hunter, about 1920.

Curtis was appalled by the treatment that the Native Americans had received at the hands of advancing white civilization. He intended his photographs to reveal the activities of a people whose lives were built around a sensitivity to the natural world.

By the time he was in his mid teens, Eric Matson and another teenager, Edith Yanktiss, had become employees of the photographic department. Eventually Matson and Yanktiss married, took over the photographic department, and reorganized it as the Matson Photo Service. For some 33 years, until Edith's death, the couple worked together taking thousands of photographs of the peoples of the Middle East.

They captured almost every aspect of these people's lives—their many different occupations, their tribal customs, and their religious ceremonies. They also produced compelling photographs of street and alley life in and around the region. Many of their depictions were of men, women, and children whose customs and dress were little removed from biblical times, as in their picture of shepherds watching their flock.

In their determination to capture images of the diverse peoples of the world, many photographers, in the last half of the

19th and the early decades of the 20th centuries, sacrificed years of their lives and, in several cases, their health as well. Perhaps the greatest effort was that exerted by Edward S. Curtis, who compiled the most extensive photographic record of Native Americans. While other photographers of Native Americans focused on one or two tribes or on the various tribes in a specific region, Curtis was determined to photograph all the tribes that he could reach. He estimated that his monumental project would take 15 years. It wound up consuming 30 years of his life.

Curtis's undertaking required considerable financial support, which he found in funding supplied by one of the world's richest men, the industrialist and banker J. Pierpont Morgan. Armed with this financing, Curtis visited more than 80 tribes and took more than 40,000 photographs. He gained the confidence of each of the tribes by spending months studying its history and customs before attempting to photograph its members. Working with a large 14-by-17-inch camera, he captured both portraits and scenes of the Native Americans' dwellings, dress, customs, and rituals.

Curtis's work brought him high praise, but he also received significant criticism. In several instances, particularly in photographing the tribes of the Pacific Northwest, he dressed the Native Americans in wigs and provided them with other trappings of their earlier days that had vanished in the face of the intruding white civilization. It was a practice that disturbed those who felt that in doing so Curtis had falsified his representation of the Native Americans. Curtis's reply was that his only interest was in presenting the first Americans as they were before their way of life had been destroyed by those coveting their lands. It was one of the first instances when the reality of the camera's ability to misrepresent as well as reveal became an issue.

Despite the criticism, Curtis's overall achievement cannot be discounted. Nor can the fact that he was a true artist with the camera. His photograph of a Native American rice gatherer, for example, reveals his flair for posing his subjects in the most dramatic manner possible. The way in which he used the long spikes of the natural growth to frame the woman in the canoe reveals his masterful sense of composition as well as his determination to ennoble a vanishing race of people.

Between 1907 and 1930 Curtis published his photographs, along with text, in a 20-volume set of books titled *The North American Indians*. When it was completed, the *New York Herald* hailed the achievement

as "the most gigantic undertaking in the publishing of books since the King James edition of the Bible." Edward S. Curtis's dream of delivering to the world an extensive, personal portrayal of a unique people and a special way of life had been realized.

By overcoming the many technical and physical challenges that confronted them, the 19th-century and early 20th-century photographers who took the world as their canvas made vital contributions. By increasing man's awareness of distant people and far-off places they shrunk the globe. In the process they blazed a whole new trail. The millions of amateur and professional photographers who today have made the taking of pictures far from home one of the most common photographic experiences follow in the footsteps of these accomplished pioneers.

Elizabeth Ellen Roberts. Young woman at a water pump, North Dakota, 1900.

Some of the most compelling pictures have been taken by amateur photographers whose work has gone practically unnoticed. Very little is known about Roberts, but her photographs tell the lively story of the pioneers of the American West.

Revealing the World in Pictures

For much of history, extensive travel has been available only to the very wealthy. Even though the end of the 19th century saw the beginning of middle-class tourism, most people obtained their visions of far-flung people and places from pictures. Photographs had the advantage over engravings of providing "scientific" proof of unknown lands while also having the potential for artistic merit. Encouraged by developments that had made camera equipment more portable and lightweight and by an eager audience at home, scores of photographers—many of them amateurs—set out at the turn of the 20th century to create a visual record of the world.

Horace A. Latimer.
A Water Carrier—Cuba, 1902.

Photographer unknown.
Chinese women suffering punishment, about 1900.

Photographer unknown.
African cliff dwellings, about 1900.

Photographer unknown.
Elephant ride in India, about 1900.

Photographer unknown.
Couple in Ireland, about 1900.

John Dunmore and George Critcherson.
Sailing Ships in an Ice Field, Labrador, Canada, 1869.

Chapter Four
Photography as Art

By the last quarter of the 19th century, photographers around the world had supplied ample proof of the camera's unique ability to record people and places. At the same time, there were others who were taking pictures for a different purpose. Convinced that the camera could be used to go beyond simply recording what was in front of the lens, these photographers, both amateur and professional, were determined to produce images of artistic merit. Believing that photographs could be every bit as beautiful and intriguing as paintings, they pursued a simply stated goal. Their aim was to convince art critics, other photographers, and the general public that photography should be regarded as a legitimate form of art.

The photographs that these early artistic photographers produced were often little different from paintings. At the time, people regarded the world's great paintings as the highest form of visual art. It was only natural that artistic photographers began by trying to produce the same kinds of images as those created by the greatest artists. They chose the same types of themes, settings, and compositions. Like painters, they emphasized the

contrasts between dark and light tones (called chiaroscuro). Many focused almost exclusively on simple but lovely, often sentimental, subjects. Some portrayed characters and incidents in fables, myths, or the Bible, while others attempted to create genre images, pictures that showed people and moments from everyday life. Still others, in the style of well-known painters, created allegorical photographs. (In an allegory, the figures represent universal human traits—such as heroism, chastity, envy, lust, or despair—not specific individuals.)

Perhaps the most distinguishing characteristic of this early artistic movement was the way in which many photographers manipulated their images. Working much like painters, they used various techniques to alter their pictures so as to make them look as much as possible like paintings, pastel or charcoal drawings, etchings, or engravings. In the process they created entirely new printing techniques and new types of photographs that expanded the concept of what a photograph was.

The artistic approach was one that had been employed by a few photographers in the years immediately following the

Alvin Langdon Coburn. *The Bridge, Venice,* 1908.

Coburn, who started photographing when he was eight years old, was an important member of the movement known as pictorialism that brought many innovations to photography. "I do not think," stated Coburn, "we have even begun to realize the possibilities of the camera."

Henry Peach Robinson. *Fading Away,* 1858.

Robinson, with the aid of his staff, made 200 prints of this picture before attaining one that satisfied him. A photographic critic of Robinson's time called the photograph "an exquisite picture of a painful subject."

medium's invention. As discussed in Chapter 2, the portraits taken by David Octavius Hill and Robert Adamson were marked by the way Hill deliberately posed their subjects and used natural light in a manner designed to make their images look as much like paintings as simple portraits. But it was in the late 1850s, slightly less than 20 years after the daguerreotype was introduced, that the full-scale movement toward creating photographs as art began.

The two men generally credited with pioneering the art photography movement were the English photographers Oscar Rejlander and Henry Peach Robinson. Before moving to Great Britain, the Swedish-born Rejlander lived in Rome, where he supported himself by copying the work of famous artists. In the early 1850s, he learned photography and decided to make it his main mode of creative expression. Almost from the moment he became a photographer, Rejlander began experimenting with new techniques. At the heart of these experiments was his desire to build upon the work of others who had introduced a new method of creating photographs. These photographers, most

notably the Frenchman Gustave Le Gray, had made what were called composite prints by printing two different negatives together on the same piece of paper to produce a single, combined image. Rejlander took this technique much farther, increasing the number of negatives he used. His first significant art picture, exhibited in 1857, when it created a sensation, used more than 30 different negatives and took six weeks to produce. It was so large—16 inches tall and 31 inches long—that two sheets of paper had to be pasted together to make the composite print. Originally titled *Hope in Repentance,* it became famous under the name *The Two Ways of Life.* It was photography's first major allegorical picture.

Rejlander's contemporary, Henry Peach Robinson, was also a painter turned photographer. Like Rejlander, Robinson's main goal was to tell a story with his camera, and he too decided that the most effective way to do this was through composite prints. Robinson's first and best-known composite art image, produced in 1858, was titled *Fading Away.* Made from five separate negatives, it was a picture of a dying young girl propped up in a chair in her family's parlor while her mother and sister look sadly on. Robinson, a master at composition, added to the emotion of the scene by placing an image of the girl's fiancé looking out of a window at the center of the picture, his back turned to hide his tears.

Along with producing many other sentimental pictures and purported genre scenes that were popular with both the public and critics, Robinson wrote several books that were among the first publications to both praise and describe the techniques of artistic photography. The first of these books, *Pictorial Effect in Photography,* published in 1869, led to the widespread use of the term *pictorial* to describe the photography-as-art approach. The movement itself was known as pictorialism. Robinson attracted many followers (although within the entire field of photography the art movement was comparatively small), and a large number of artistic photographs, many of them created out of the photographers' imaginations, were produced. Many of these pictures were overly sentimental or overly imitative of paintings and spawned a strong negative reaction from an opposing group of photographers.

The person who led the revolt against pictorialism was Peter Henry Emerson. Born in 1856 in Cuba, where his American father and English mother owned sugar plantations, Emerson was a distant cousin of the American writer Ralph Waldo Emerson. He attended school in the United States, then went to college in England, where he studied to become a doctor. He received his degree and made England his home, but never practiced medicine. Instead, from 1885 on he devoted himself to

---

Platinum Prints

From the 1850s through the mid 1890s, the standard paper for making photographic prints was albumen paper, so called because it was prepared with egg whites. (It was replaced by gelatin-emulsion paper, like the photographic paper used today.) Albumen paper, which produced an image composed of silver, was invented by Louis Désiré Blanquart-Evrard in 1850. Soon paper coated with albumen was being sold by dozens of manufacturers. The paper was so popular that in order to keep up with demand, Germany's Dresden Albuminizing Company, the largest in the world, used some 60,000 eggs a day.

In 1880, however, a new process was introduced that produced print images of platinum rather than silver. They were known as platinum prints or platinotypes. The new process was invented by an Englishman, William Willis. He produced his special type of printing material by coating paper with potassium chloroplatinate and ferric oxylate. After the coating was dry, the paper was contact-printed with a negative, by sunlight, in the usual manner. The print was developed in potassium oxylate, fixed with a solution of hydrochloric or citric acid, and then washed.

When Willis put his new type of paper on the market through his Platinotype Company, the product was eagerly adopted by scores of artistic photographers. It was considerably more expensive than albumen paper, but the prints it produced were more delicate in tone, with a slightly pinkish cast, and were far less apt to fade than most previous—or later—types of photographs. Pictorial and naturalist photographers alike welcomed this new and beautiful material. Peter Henry Emerson was effusive in his praise of platinum images. "For low-toned effects and for the greyday landscapes," he stated, "the platinotype process is unequalled."

Emerson, in fact, felt so strongly about what the platinum print had brought to photography that he boldly stated that if the platinotype process were ever to become a lost art he "would never take another photograph."

Frederick Evans shared Emerson's passion for the long, delicate tonal scale made possible by platinum paper, but when he could no longer afford it, Evans in fact gave up his photographic career rather than use what he considered to be lesser-quality materials. In the late 1930s the paper became so expensive to manufacture that it disappeared from the market. But in the years that platinum paper was available, it permitted scores of photographers, most notably including Edward Weston and Paul Strand, to produce images of great sensitivity and beauty. In modern times, certain photographers such as George Tice and Irving Penn have hand-prepared platinum paper and have used it for making prints for exhibition purposes.

---

photography, for which he had developed a passion during his college years. Emerson loved nature, particularly the English countryside, and most of his photographs were of simple scenes such as farming, hay gathering, duck shooting, and peaceful river travel.

Emerson wrote many articles and a major book in which he declared that photography had the potential to be artistically superior to any other visual medium. He also wrote that beautiful photographs should be framed and mounted in the same manner as fine paintings. Up to this time photographs were rarely hung on the walls of private homes. Instead, they were kept as individual mounted prints in an album or portfolio, and commonly were placed one

Peter Henry Emerson. *Poling the Marsh Hay,* about 1885.

Emerson had unbending beliefs about how artistic photographs should be produced. One of his strongest convictions was that photographers should develop their negatives on the same day they were taken so that the mental impression of what they wished to achieve in each picture would still be fresh in their minds.

at a time on an easel in the owner's drawing room or parlor for viewing. But due to Emerson's influence, this began to change.

Emerson's book, titled *Naturalistic Photography for Students of the Art,* was intended to counteract pictorialism's insistence that art consisted primarily of pictures created out of photographers' imaginations. He stated his main thesis this way: "Whenever the artist has been true to Nature, art has been good; whenever the artist has neglected Nature and followed his imagination, there has resulted bad art. Nature, then, should be the artist's standard." Emerson gave the term *naturalism* to this approach to artistic photography. It became the foundation of what is now termed purist or straight artistic photography.

A highly opinionated and difficult man, Emerson was often openly and harshly critical of his fellow photographers. He was vehemently opposed to the composite print and all other kinds of manipulation in printing, which he considered to be photographic trickery, and he made Oscar

Rejlander and Henry Peach Robinson the targets of some of his most caustic verbal attacks. It was one of the ironies of photography that this bombastic individual produced many of the most tranquil and beautiful of all the early artistic photographs. His talent for using very simple, commonplace subjects in peaceful settings is evidenced in his photograph *Poling the Marsh Hay.* By placing the woman prominently in the foreground and revealing the hay-gathering activities as a backdrop he created the peaceful image he sought. The soft focus of most of the photograph adds to its appeal.

Emerson thought a photograph should be focused at one point, with other things being less sharp because, he argued, that is the way the eye sees things. He was actually wrong in this belief, because he did not take into account the fact that we rapidly and unconsciously scan a real scene, seeing point after point sharply, thus building an impression of total sharpness. In this he misunderstood a fundamental aspect of the new and highly influential movement in painting called impressionism, which he greatly admired. Although the overall mood and style of his work often looks much the same to our eyes as that of pictorialist images of the same period, Emerson did not arrange or artificially pose his subjects or use any techniques to imitate the appearance of a painting. His seeing and his methods were straightforward; he strove honestly to show the beauty of the subject in its own terms, not his subjective interpretation of it.

Another English photographer who shared Emerson's passion for nature as a subject was Frank Meadow Sutcliffe. He

inherited much of his creative talent from his father, who was a painter, etcher, printer, and amateur photographer. In 1875, Sutcliffe's family moved to the town of Whitby, Yorkshire, where he began his photographic career. Whitby was situated on the English seacoast; its location provided Sutcliffe with the subject matter for most of his photographs. He captured images of harbor life, of boats putting out to sea and returning to shore, of women cleaning or selling fish, and of fishermen mending their nets, baiting their hooks, or spending time chatting with their fellow seamen. He was particularly fascinated by the children who spent so much of their time at the harbor or along the shore. He photographed them bathing and splashing in the water, climbing upon boats, and watching the fishermen and peddlers at work.

To Sutcliffe, these subjects presented the opportunity to portray what for him was a very special type of life. More important, he saw in them the settings and simple activities for creating images that would be as picturesque as the finest paintings.

The peaceful scenes that Sutcliffe continually encountered were charming by nature. But it was his special photographic talents that allowed him to transfer this charm to his images. He did not believe in posing his subjects, because he thought the resulting photographs would be too artificial, and he had the patience to wait as long as it took to capture whatever picture he was taking in the most appealing way. The photographs he produced were beautifully balanced, marked by the way he was able to frame the main subjects in the center of his images with inanimate or human subjects

Frank Sutcliffe. *Water Rats*, 1886.

When this photograph of boys jumping in and out of the sea without any clothes on was first exhibited, Sutcliffe was actually excommunicated, or excluded, from his church. He overcame this disapproval and became recognized as a master of both light and composition.

George Davison. *Berkshire Teams and Teamsters,* about 1888.

Davison concentrated on capturing images of rural scenes. Like many pictorialists, he often presented a romanticized view of his subjects.

on each side of the picture. However, he was essentially a pictorialist in his taste in printing, often manipulating the print to add atmospheric haze or create a somewhat impressionistic appearance.

Sutcliffe's images earned him much acclaim, but the early pictorialist movement continued to be the subject of criticism, particularly from those who felt that photography was becoming too imitative of paintings. Disturbed by this criticism, a group of influential English photographers banded together to spread their beliefs around the world. In 1891 they founded an organization which they named the Linked Ring. They chose this name because to them it symbolized their stated purpose of "linking those who are interested in the development of the highest form of Art of which Photography is capable." From its beginnings, the Linked Ring had enormous influence in photographic circles both in Europe and America. Eventually it became the inspiration for an even more powerful group that would be formed in

the United States. The American group was known as the Photo-Secession.

One of the founding members of the Linked Ring was the English photographer George Davison. He, like both the naturalist Emerson and the early pictorialists, was a great admirer of impressionist paintings, particularly the way in which impressionist artists concentrated on capturing the changing effects of light as they appeared to the human eye. Much like their paintings, Davison's images were marked by his deliberate contrast of shadow and light, shadings that appear as if they were created by the stroke of a brush rather than with a camera. This approach can perhaps best be seen in the photograph Davison titled both *Berkshire Teams and Teamsters* and *Part of Day.* In this picture, Davison captured the atmosphere created by a darkening sky signifying day's end. The light created by the fading sun shining through both dark and white billowing clouds and the shadows cast by the horses and men in the image make the figures appear almost as if they were taken in silhouette. By framing the lone figure in the center of the picture with the men and horses to either side, Davison gave a pleasing balance to the picture.

Thanks to the influence of photographers like Davison, and to organizations like the Linked Ring, the pictorial movement spread throughout Europe. In France, a photographer named Robert Demachy not only adopted the approach but helped pioneer a technique that would be employed by artistic photographers everywhere.

As a young man Demachy was most interested in music and in driving fast cars. He was a successful banker with esthetic interests. Before he turned to photography in 1892, he was a literary critic and an amateur painter. He particularly admired the work of the renowned artist Edgar Degas, who was himself an amateur photographer as well as a professional painter. Degas was taken with the motion studies that Eadweard Muybridge had produced (see page 18). He made many drawings from Muybridge's pictures, including a lineup of ballet dancers in various postures, drawn to give the appearance of motion. Several of Demachy's photographs are highly reminiscent of Degas' paintings.

Demachy believed that in order to produce a work of art the photographer had to regard the photograph he or she took as just the first step in creating a masterful image. The key, he was convinced, were the techniques and manipulations the photographer would then use to add to and change the photographic image. Demachy was a pioneer and a master in the use of the gum bichromate printing process. A negative was contact printed on paper coated with an emulsion of gum arabic, potassium bichromate, and any color of pigment. Light passed strongly through the thinnest parts of the negative, which were the dark areas of the subject, and less strongly through the middle-tone and highlight areas. The emulsion hardened in proportion to the strength of the light, so when the print was developed in warm water the emulsion would wash away in the lighter areas, letting more of the white (or colored) paper show through, but it would remain more strongly in the middle-tone and darker areas of the positive image. The emulsion could be applied evenly, or with coarse brushstrokes, or stippled on, for a variety of effects. And the photographer could use very hot water to wash away or alter any details in the print he desired. It was a process that allowed Demachy and other pictorialists to work much like painters.

Demachy's photographs placed him at the forefront of those who sought artistry in their pictures by manipulating their images. He wrote five books and more than 1,000 articles describing all of the various aspects of photographic manipulation. He also traveled throughout the world, lecturing on the subject.

In the last two decades of the 1800s, the art photography movement in Europe gained great momentum. Much of it was due to the appearance of the first photographic exhibitions devoted exclusively to the work of pictorialist photographers. The first of these exhibitions, featuring images by Peter Henry Emerson, was mounted in Vienna in 1887 by the Club-der-Amateur Photographers. In the words of one of the club's founders, it marked "the first time

Robert Demachy. *Behind the Scenes,* about 1900.

Young ballet dancers were among Demachy's favorite subjects. Often he would manipulate a negative, develop it, and then apply further manipulations to the negative and develop it again. As a result, he often produced very different looking photographs from the same negative.

Baron Adolphe de Meyer. *Still Life*, about 1906.

The still life, a traditional subject for painting, also became a theme for photographers. De Meyer was a leading Photo-Secessionist who would later make his mark as arguably the world's first great fashion photographer.

that art-lovers had been offered a series of original photographs of interest not in the objects they represent, but in the interpretation and handling." Four years later, the club astounded both the art and photographic worlds by presenting a massive exhibition of 600 pictorial photographs selected from more than 4,000 candidates.

In 1893, three other major pictorial exhibitions took place in Europe. The Linked Ring mounted what would become an annual series of artistic photography shows. Robert Demachy and the English photographer Alfred Maskell presented an exhibition of prints they had made using the gum-bichromate process. And the Kunsthalle Museum in Hamburg, Germany, organized a First International Exhibition of Amateur Photographers. If the art world had been astounded by the

huge Club-der-Amateur Photographers show of 1891, it was positively stunned by the Kunsthalle Museum's display of 6,000 artistic photographs. One of the added features of this show was a demonstration of how to frame photographs properly according to the tastes of the period.

The attention that artistic photography received through the growing number of pictorialist exhibitions had a dramatic effect on the many European photographic clubs made up of both amateurs and professionals. When The Photo-Club de Paris staged its First Exhibition of Photographic Art, the show took on an importance that went beyond the exhibition itself. By this time, the process for reproducing photographs on a printed page had been invented (described in Chapter 6), and as an accompaniment to the exhibition the club issued a booklet containing reproductions of 50 of the photographs displayed in the show. It was a forerunner to the illustrated catalog that is now a regular part of almost all major photographic exhibitions.

By the beginning of the 1900s, artistic photography had gained a solid foothold in Europe. However, it was in the United States that pictorialism came to full flower. Much of it was due to the contributions of one man. His name was Alfred Stieglitz; he became legendary not only for the photographs he took but for the organization he founded, the galleries he established, and the two publications he edited. It was through all of these that Stieglitz introduced the work of scores of fellow American and foreign pictorial photographers to the world, and introduced the newest developments in modern art to the United States.

VOL. I.   NO. 3.

CAMERA NOTES

OFFICIAL ORGAN OF
THE CAMERA CLUB, N.Y.

PER YEAR $1.00

PUBLISHED BY
THE CAMERA CLUB, N.Y.
111-113 WEST 38TH STREET
NEW YORK CITY

Edited by Alfred Stieglitz, the journal Camera Notes *brought the work of many of the earliest pictorialists to the attention of the public. Published from 1897 to 1903, it also contained articles written by leading Photo-Secessionists and critics.*

Born in Hoboken, New Jersey, Stieglitz received his university education in Germany, where he studied engineering. He learned some of the technical principles of photography in a physics and chemistry course, but his involvement in photography really began only after he spotted an inexpensive camera in a shop window in Berlin and purchased it. After taking only a few pictures he realized that he was much more interested in photography than he was in pursuing an engineering career.

When he returned to the United States, Stieglitz was amazed to find how popular photography had become since he had left for Europe. He was particularly taken with the artistic approach that an increasing number of American photographers were beginning to take. He felt, however, that these photographers were not gaining the recognition that they deserved. In 1886 he joined the Camera Club of New York. He soon became editor of the club's journal and turned it into a publication titled *Camera Notes*. In its pages Stieglitz published photographs by pictorialists from both the United States and abroad. The journal also contained articles extolling the virtues of artistic photography and describing its various characteristics.

Although *Camera Notes* soon became the nation's leading champion of pictorialism, Stieglitz was upset with the way that certain members of the camera club were voicing their opposition to the movement. In 1902 he resigned from the club and he and a group of other photographers founded an organization they called the Photo-Secession. They chose that name because to them it meant a breaking away from all previous subject-oriented photographic movements.

Soon after its founding, the organization introduced its own publication, called *Camera Work*. For the next 15 years, Stieglitz edited and personally solicited all the images for the journal, establishing it as the most widely read photographic publication of its day. Stieglitz and other members of the Photo-Secession also opened what became one of America's most important art galleries. Its official name was The Little Galleries of the Photo-Secession, but it was commonly referred to as "291," since it was located at 291 Fifth Avenue in New York City. The gallery proudly displayed the

Alfred Stieglitz. Photo-Secession exhibition, 1906.

The Little Galleries of the Photo-Secession became one of the most visited photographic galleries in the United States. Its permanent exhibitions included the work of leading pictorialists from around the world.

Alfred Stieglitz. *Paula,* 1899.

Stieglitz's mastery of light and shadow marks most of his photographs. "Photography," stated Stieglitz, "is my passion. The search for truth my obsession."

paintings and sculptures by artists whose work featured new techniques in visual expression. Among these artists were Europeans such as Pablo Picasso, Georges Braque, Paul Cessna, and Auguste Rodin, and Americans such as Georgia O'Keeffe, John Marin, and Arthur Dove. Modern art was the primary feature of two later galleries that Stieglitz operated in the 1920s and 1930s.

In his own photography, Stieglitz evolved from his early pictorialist style to an uncompromising straight approach that characterizes his finest work. He recognized this development in others too, and gave Paul Strand—who was to become one of the major American photographic artists of the 20th century—his first major exhibition, at 291.

Alfred Stieglitz was always on the hunt for photographic talent. One of his earliest discoveries, at the beginning of the Photo-Secession, was a young man destined to become as famous as Stieglitz himself. His name was Edward Steichen. As a young man in Milwaukee, Wisconsin, Steichen studied painting. When his father gave him a camera, however, he discovered a new passion. Although he continued to paint for most of the rest of his life, his main efforts went into photography. His photographic contributions were so great that he would eventually became known as the "dean of American photographers."

Edward Steichen conquered almost every field of photography. His pictorial images made him one of the leading lights of the Photo-Secession. Many of his portraits were hailed as true masterpieces. He became one of the giants of both advertising

work of established pictorialists and introduced the images of still-unheralded artistic photographers.

Through its art gallery and its publications the Photo-Secession profoundly influenced photography in America and abroad. Pictorialists, both amateur and professional, flocked to 291, regarding it almost as a shrine. The organization's greatest impact was perhaps felt most keenly in photographic clubs throughout the nation. Inspired by the Photo-Secession, many of these clubs encouraged their members even more passionately than their counterparts in Europe to take up pictorialism and held regular exhibitions of these members' work. The rediscovered work of Hill and Adamson, and photographs by Julia Margaret Cameron were shown in special exhibits at 291. In addition, 291 was the first gallery in the United States to show

and fashion photography. As a Signal Corps cameraman during World War I he captured outstanding war images. Commissioned a lieutenant commander in World War II, he was in charge of all of the United States Navy's combat photography in the Pacific theater of war.

Aside from his own photographic accomplishments, Steichen was also a curator of photography. From 1947 to 1962 he served as director of photography at New York's Museum of Modern Art. The museum had established a department of photography under the direction of Beaumont Newhall in 1930, some ten years before many other major nongovernment museums started adding photographs to their collections. Under Steichen's direction in the years after World War II, the Museum of Modern Art became one of the world's most important photographic repositories. While at the museum, Steichen organized the "Family of Man," the most popular photographic exhibition ever held. From 1952 to 1955 he traveled the world seeking the most outstanding images available for the project. When mounted, the exhibition included those photographs he had selected from more than 2 million candidates. Eventually, the "Family of Man" was viewed by more than 9 million people in 69 different countries. A book based on the exhibition has been the best-selling photographic book of all time.

Perhaps more than those of any other American pictorialist, Steichen's early artistic photographs are reminiscent of the paintinglike images produced by Peter Henry Emerson, George Davison, and Frank Sutcliffe. Typical of these images is Steichen's *Flatiron—Evening,* a gum bichromate print. It is a photograph marked by its soft, almost ethereal quality. The contrast of the fragile tree limbs in the foreground of the picture with the massive building in the background, and the dark shadows accentuated by occasional splashes of light distinguish the picture as a masterful artistic rendering.

Gertrude Käsebier, like Edward Steichen, was another of Alfred Stieglitz's outstanding protégés. As was the case with many pictorialists, her work was marked by the way she expressed her own deepest feelings and emotions through her images. Influenced by having grown up on the American prairie, Käsebier was a strong

Edward Steichen. *Flatiron— Evening,* 1905.

At the beginning of the 20th century, the Flatiron Building in New York City was one of the most commonly photographed of all structures. Steichen's is the best-known image of the triangular-shaped building.

Gertrude Käsebier. *Blessed Art Thou Among Women*, 1899.

Käsebier was one of a number of women Photo-Secessionists who made their mark by producing artistic photographs. She also ran a professional portrait studio in New York.

advocate of the growing early 19th-century American belief that, rather than be coddled, children should be encouraged to develop a sense of independence. She expressed this conviction in many of her photographs, particularly in her image *Blessed Art Thou Among Women,* which became one of the best known of all pictorialist images.

Almost all of the techniques employed by those who sought to bring art to their photographs can be seen in this picture, which, in several ways, is allegorical in nature. The child stands at the threshold of a doorway, which implies that a major development in her life is about to occur. Her dark clothing contrasts dramatically with the all-white garment of the adult woman, who may be her mother, a guardian, or even an angel. The soft, warm tonal scale is the result of the platinum process used for the print. The pose of the subjects is simple and direct. But Käsebier's message is also clear. By having the adult's hand placed on the child's shoulder, she shows the woman to be supportive and encouraging of the youngster. At the same time, by depicting the woman's face in profile while presenting the child looking boldly ahead of her, Käsebier tells us that this is a girl being encouraged to act and think for herself.

The fact that photography has never stagnated has been due to the vision and influence of photographers of all kinds. Particularly important has been the presence of successful photographers who have devoted much of their time to passing on their skills to young men and women seeking to follow in their footsteps.

One of the most influential teachers of photography was a shy, highly intelligent man from Ohio named Clarence H. White. After spending several years as a bookkeeper, White began taking his first photographs in 1894. Although Ohio was far removed from the center of Photo-Secession activities in New York, he became enthralled with the photographs he encountered in *Camera Work* and joined the Photo-Secession.

In his pictures, White concentrated on simple, innocent domestic scenes. He captured images of youngsters playing childhood games and people caught in the midst of peaceful reflection. Among White's most intriguing photographs is that titled *Drops of Rain*. In this typically soft-focused image, White depicted a young boy gazing into a glass globe, that object embraced by the Photo-Secessionists as the symbol of their movement.

Aside from his photographs, White's greatest contribution to the medium came through his teaching. From 1907 to 1925 he taught photography at Columbia University. He was such an effective teacher that aspiring photographers traveled from all corners of the nation to take his courses. Among his students, many of whom credited him for launching their photographic careers, were such future masters of the medium as Dorothea Lange, Margaret Bourke-White, Doris Ulmann, and Paul Outerbridge. White was also the first president of the Pictorial Photographers of America, an organization which, like the Photo-Secession, played a key role in gaining acceptance of photography as an art form.

Although the Photo-Secession captured so much attention and produced so many

Clarence White. *Drops of Rain,* about 1902.

White was a master at capturing those he photographed in soft, natural light. The glass globe was regarded by the Photo-Secessionists as a symbol of beauty and the many mysteries of life.

outstanding images and imaginative photographic talents, its glory days were relatively short. One of the reasons was that the pictorialist approach of most of its members was regarded by many critics as a mere imitation of paintings. Alfred Stieglitz himself was the cause of a number of photographers abandoning the movement. Many photographers felt that Stieglitz, who was often dictatorial, played favorites in his selection of those whose work was published in *Camera Work* and exhibited in the Photo-Secession gallery.

The coming of World War I, with its terrible toll of death and destruction, also played a major role in pictorialism's decline.

Suddenly the simple, innocent, charming life that had been the subject of so many artistic photographs seemed out of touch with the real world.

But the decline of 19th- and early 20th-century pictorialism did not mean that art photography was abandoned. Far from it. Beginning in the 1920s, scores of photographers took up where the early pictorialists had left off by adopting bold new approaches.

These new art photographers eschewed soft-focus effects in favor of much sharper images. Most of all, they created whole new forms of photography such as the photogram and the photomontage. Two men

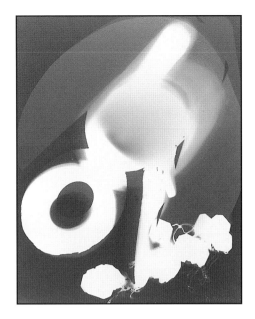

Man Ray. *Rayograph,* about 1924.

Man Ray's photograms were a result of his desire to expand the boundaries of photography. He stated that his work "is designed to amuse, bewilder, annoy, or inspire reflections. . . . The streets are full of admirable craftsmen, but so few dreamers."

László Moholy-Nagy. *Berlin Radio Tower,* about 1925.

Along with creating photomontages, Moholy-Nagy was most interested in taking photographs from angles that revealed the patterns and shapes created by light playing upon natural and man-made objects.

often regarded as fathers of avant-garde art photography were the American Man Ray and the Hungarian László Moholy-Nagy.

Man Ray's avowed purpose was to free photography from the mechanics of the medium, even, in fact, to free it from the camera. He accomplished this by positioning objects on chemically treated paper. He then exposed the areas around the objects by placing them under very strong light. The result was evocative silhouette-type images commonly called photograms, but Man Ray called them "Rayographs."

Moholy-Nagy was one of the founding faculty of the Bauhaus, a university of modern architecture and design in Germany from 1919 to 1933. In the course he taught on light, film, and photography, students created photograms and experimented with another kind of artistic image

making called photomontage. Pioneered by Raoul Hausmann and Hannah Hoch in 1918 and 1919, a photomontage is a modern combination image. It uses individual elements from several different photographs, and often words or phrases from printed sources to construct a complex, often abstract image. The separate elements may be cut or torn out of the source material, pasted together, and rephotographed, or they may be brought together by combination printing, as in early pictorialism. Hand-drawn or painted elements are often incorporated as well.

The photogram and the photomontage were but the beginning of a whole new impetus toward photography as art known as modernism. "The once popular 'storytelling' pictures, the tender landscapes with sheep, the bowls of flowers, the portraits of little children have had to make way for prints in which a new and almost disordered spirit is evident," wrote the editor of *Vanity Fair* magazine.

This approach, which broke new ground not only in the content of artistic photographs but in how they were taken, could be seen in the work of the Russian photographer Alexander Rodchenko. Originally a sculptor and a painter, Rodchenko was one of the pioneers of constructionism, an abstract style of both painting and photography that placed the design of a picture above its content. He was also a champion of taking pictures from extreme angles of view, a photographic technique eventually adopted by scores of mid-20th-century photographers. Most photographers viewed their subjects head-on, commonly with a reflex-viewing camera held at waist level or

Barbara Morgan.
*Spring on Madison
Square*, 1938.

*Influenced by the work of
Man Ray, Morgan creat-
ed scores of intriguing
photomontages. A versa-
tile photographer, she also
became known for dra-
matic images of dancers
in performance.*

a 35mm camera held at eye level. Rod-chenko added dramatically to the artistic effects of his pictures by photographing in a bold new way. "In photography," he stated, "there is the old point of view, the angle of vision of a man [with a waist-level camera] who stands on the ground and looks straight ahead, or as I call it, makes 'belly-button' shots. . . . I fight this point of view, and will fight it along with my colleagues in the new photography. The most inter-esting angle shots today are those 'down from above' and 'up from below,' and their diagonals." Rodchenko photographed from windows, balconies, stairways, ladders, and even trees to get extreme overhead views, and laid on the ground or otherwise placed the camera very low to get dynamic upward-looking angles.

By the 1930s and early 1940s, the new art photography had gained wide accep-tance. Regular exhibitions of modernist works were increasingly held and were well attended. At the same time, photographers such as Edward Weston and Paul Strand (see Chapter 9) applied their purist or straight approach to producing images of great artis-tic merit. It became clear that rather than dying out with the end of the Photo-Seces-sion, art photography had not only survived but had taken photography in exciting new directions. The fact that photographs are today proudly displayed alongside paintings, sculpture, and other works of art in muse-ums and galleries throughout the world pro-vides testimony to the achievements of both the early pictorialists and those who extend-ed their vision.

Chapter Five

Documentary Photography

A t the same time that those who were determined to gain acceptance for photography as an art form were first beginning to produce their images, other men and women, who came to be known as documentary photographers, were using their cameras to record people, places, and conditions more powerfully than ever before. Photohistorians have commonly placed the work of documentary photographers into two categories, *straight documentary* and *social documentary*. Both categories involve photographs of clearly defined groups of people and the conditions in which they live, but with differences in emphasis and intent. Straight documentary refers to pictures taken to capture specific ways of life before they have vanished from an ever-changing world. Often the photographer engages in some degree of interpretation by using a distinct style of composition and printing to enhance the appeal or interest of the pictures.

Social documentary pictures deal with a specific social subgroup—coal miners of Appalachia, agricultural workers in a drought area, people in a nursing home or retirement center, members of an inner-city gang, for example. The photographs concentrate on the individuals and the specific things they

do, or are unable to do, to deal with the immediate problems of their lives. There is sometimes an impression that social documentary deals only with negative conditions and experiences, things that need to be reformed. However, much social documentary work has the positive intent of making viewers aware of good and successful social conditions and programs that deserve support and encouragement.

Of all photographers, social documentarians feel an obligation to be as truthful as possible about their subjects. Of course, the choice of what to show and what to leave out, from how close or far away, and from what angle of view may be influenced by unconscious preferences and dislikes. But the photographers make every effort to avoid injecting personal interpretation. They try to select the details and information that present the real situation truthfully and objectively.

Straight documentary photography has dealt with a wide range of lifestyles and people. Among the straight documentary photographers was a woman named Frances Benjamin Johnston. A niece of Mrs. Grover Cleveland, she was allowed within the White House, where she took pictures of President

Dorothea Lange, shown here in 1934, was one of the world's leading documentary photographers. "There is no real warfare between the artist and the documentary photographer," she wrote. "He has to be both . . . the documentary photographer is trying to speak to you in terms of everybody's experience."

Lewis Hine. *Young boys in coal mine*, about 1910 (top).

Joseph Byron. *Harrison Grey Fiske Dinner*, 1900 (bottom).

Documentary photographers trained their cameras on both ends of the social spectrum. Hine's picture shows child laborers working from dawn to dusk sorting coal, miles underground. Byron spent most of his career photographing the lives of the wealthy, such as this group of business tycoons enjoying a lavish banquet in New York City.

was then little more than 50 years old, she obtained a commission from the officials of the Paris Exposition of 1900 to record how the system was working. The images she captured of Washington, D.C., schoolchildren inside their classrooms and on various field trips provided not only a dramatic portrayal of the free American school system at work but revealed Johnston's artistry with a camera.

Her photographs were among the most highly acclaimed of those shown at the Paris Exposition and earned her several other commissions. Among them was one she received from African-American leader Booker T. Washington, which would lead to her most important work.

Washington, a former slave, invited Johnston to travel to the South to record life at Hampton Institute in Virginia and Tuskegee Institute in Alabama, two schools that had been established to offer African-American students both educational courses and training in skilled trades. Almost all the parents or grandparents of these students had once been slaves. From the moment she arrived at the Hampton school, Johnston was struck by the dedication of the teachers and students she encountered. She became determined to share her appreciation of what was being accomplished through her camera.

She took scores of pictures of young men and women learning to be carpenters, milliners, cobblers, farmers, and tradespeople. At first glance, it might appear that the ambitions of these young people were not high. They were, after all, studying to be skilled laborers, not doctors or lawyers. But in segregated America, filled with severe

Cleveland and of several others who followed him in office. She also captured images of other famous people. These portraits made her one of the most successful of all early women photographers, but she became determined to expand her photographic horizons and built a career taking illustrations and writing articles on social topics for magazines and newspapers.

Aware that nations around the world were increasingly curious abut the American system of free public schooling, which

Frances Benjamin Johnston. Carpentry students at Hampton Institute, 1900.

Johnston was among the earliest and most successful of all documentary photographers. "The woman who makes photography profitable," she wrote, "must have . . . good taste, a quick eye, and a talent for detail."

racism, the education they were receiving represented their best and, in many cases, their only chance for bettering their lives.

Johnston's photographs portray the dignity with which the young people of Tuskegee and Hampton went about their studies; they also disclose the remarkable sense of composition she brought to her images. This special talent can be seen in her photograph of students learning to be carpenters. The picture as a whole is marked by a wonderful sense of balance. But as one studies the picture more closely it becomes apparent that contained within this one image are individual groupings that could stand on their own as separate images. It was a technique that Johnston employed in many of her photographs.

While Johnston was determined to reveal the accomplishments of African-

American students seeking to enrich their opportunities, another early straight documentary photographer devoted his energies to recording a unique way of life before it vanished forever. His name was Solomon Butcher. He and his family were among the early settlers of the Nebraska Territory of the American West.

Butcher was particularly fascinated with the sod houses that served as the first homes of so many families in the region where he lived. Although the Nebraska soil was among the richest in the world, it contained almost no trees from which wooden houses could be built. The soil, however, was matted with heavy grass that held it together like rubber. The inventive Nebraska pioneers cut the earth into long strips and used it like bricks to build their first homes in the West.

Solomon Butcher. Sod house family, 1886.

Although Butcher's primary intent was to preserve a vanishing way of life, he also wanted to produce masterfully composed photographs. He arranged the boys at the left of the picture by height and framed the picture by placing all the family members to the left and right of the window and door.

As more and more people poured into the region, Butcher witnessed the replacement of the sod houses by homes built of wood, carted in from distant areas. He became obsessed with capturing pictures of the "soddies," as they were called, before they became a thing of the past. Day after day he traveled the long distances between homesteads, taking photographs of the unique dwellings and of the families that lived within them.

Through Butcher's efforts, an important, vanishing type of American dwelling was preserved. But the pictures he took, such as the image above of a pioneer couple and their four sons, revealed much more than perhaps even he could have envisioned. As he asked this frontier family to pose in front of its home, they became aware that this was perhaps their one opportunity to have themselves and their belongings recorded for future generations to see. Like most of the families he photographed, they asked Butcher to wait while they hauled their proudest possessions—prized pieces of furniture, farm implements, bird cages, pets and farm animals—to the front of their dwelling so that they could be included in the picture. The result was photographic documentation not only of sod houses, but of the artifacts of life on the American frontier.

The period in which the first American documentary photographers operated, the middle to late 1800s and early 1900s, coincided with a great tide of immigration to the United States. The vast majority of these newcomers (some 30 million) came from countries throughout Europe, although many came from China and Japan as well.

The first Chinese to arrive in the United States actually made the journey before the

Arnold Genthe. *The Butcher,* about 1895.

Genthe was an extremely versatile photographer. In addition to his Chinatown photographs, such as this one, he was an accomplished portraitist who traveled extensively throughout South America and Europe, where he captured striking landscape and architectural images.

great era of immigration began. They came to California in the 1850s, seeking to strike it rich during the Gold Rush days. When they arrived, they found that strict laws against people from the Orient barred them from digging in the gold fields. Determined to remain in America, they took in washing and eked out a living in any way they could. Between 1864 and 1869, many of these Chinese found jobs with the construction crews that built the western half of the transcontinental railroad.

The prejudice that the Chinese encountered led them to band together wherever they settled in the United States. This was particularly true in San Francisco, where, suspicious of outsiders, they created a large neighborhood that outsiders called Chinatown. It was really a city within a city. Aware that Americans were curious about these people whose language, dress, and customs were so different from their own, a San Francisco photographer became determined to portray these people to the outside world.

This photographer, Arnold Genthe, had come to San Francisco from Germany to tutor the son of wealthy parents. He had been highly educated in his native country and was both an accomplished painter and musician. Almost from the moment he arrived in the United States he began his attempts to depict Chinatown's inhabitants visually. At first Genthe tried to do so through paintings, but whenever he took out his sketchpad, the people he was attempting to draw ran away. He then decided to compile his record through photographs. Once again he met with deep resistance.

The Detective or Spy Camera

The real-life images that Arnold Genthe captured in San Francisco's Chinatown are referred to as candid photographs. That is, they are informal, unposed pictures. Genthe took his pictures by keeping himself hidden from those he photographed. In the last quarter of the 19th century, inventors began to create all types of cameras which would allow photographers to take secret, candid photographs without having to hide. Known as detective or spy cameras, these devices were either disguised as everyday objects or hidden within familiar objects.

One of the earliest detective cameras was the Stirn Secret Camera, invented in 1885 by Robert Gray in New York and manufactured by the C. P. Stirn Company. The camera was worn under a vest with the lens looking through a buttonhole, and pictures were taken by pulling on a string in the user's pocket. Another early device was the Deceptive Angle Box. Its hidden lens, located on the side of the camera, allowed its user to innocently point the camera in one direction while capturing a picture of unsuspecting people who were situated off to the side. Other early detective devices included tiny cameras placed in the handles of walking sticks, in the cases of pocket watches, in innocent-looking packages, in the bindings of books, and even inside ladies' garters. One of the most popular of all these cameras was the French Photo Cravate, which featured a tiny hidden camera with its lens set into an ornamental tie pin.

The success of these secretive cameras led to even more sophisticated devices, some of which were used as spying devices in World Wars I and II. Cameras that produced clear, detailed images were inserted into matchboxes, cigarette packs, and cigarette lighters. Perhaps the most interesting of all the spy or detective devices was the Doppel Sport Pigeon Camera, developed in Germany during World War I. These cameras, equipped with automatic timers, were attached to pigeons that were to fly over enemy forces and take pictures of their position and strength. Much to the Germans' disappointment, almost all the pigeons, weighed down by the camera, crashed to earth before completing their missions.

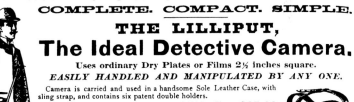

PHOTOGRAPHIC OUTFITS

COMPLETE. COMPACT. SIMPLE.

THE LILLIPUT,
The Ideal Detective Camera.

Uses ordinary Dry Plates or Films 2½ inches square.
EASILY HANDLED AND MANIPULATED BY ANY ONE.

Camera is carried and used in a handsome Sole Leather Case, with sling strap, and contains six patent double holders.
Camera complete with non-actinic Lamp and 108 Dry Plates, **$25.00**
If fitted with Film Kits and Films, - - - - **27.00**
Illustrated book of instructions with each.
THIS IS NOT A TOY, BUT A THOROUGHLY SERVICEABLE CAMERA.
Every artist or lecturer should have one to catch the many piquant views from life which they would otherwise lose with a more cumbersome or showy instrument.

Beautiful Lantern Slides can be made from these negatives, and also enlargements many times the size of the original plate.

A FEW REASONS WHY YOU SHOULD BUY A LILLIPUT.

BECAUSE of its compactness and beauty; its unlikeness in appearance to a Camera, yet being one with which you can photograph anything that could be done with any other Camera.
BECAUSE you can make pictures with it more easily than with any other Camera; because you can finish at any time one or more negatives, and see precisely what results you are obtaining.
BECAUSE the Plates are INEXPENSIVE, EASILY HANDLED and MANIPULATED by any one.
BECAUSE it can be used for either INSTANTANEOUS or TIME exposures.

E. & H. T. ANTHONY & CO.
591 Broadway, New-York.

The detective camera featured in this ad from about 1890 was but one of scores of devices invented to permit users to take pictures secretly. This particular detective camera was disguised as a simple carrying case.

Jacques-Henri Lartigue. *Delage Racer at Full Speed,* 1912.

Many of Lartigue's photographs are marked by the sense of captured motion. The contrast between the vertical figures of the bystanders in this picture and the horizontal racing car is also typical of his technique.

Genthe refused to be discouraged. He switched to a small camera which he kept inside his pocket. By hiding in doorways or behind poles or signs, he managed to capture his subjects unaware by unobtrusively taking out his camera, shooting the picture, and slipping the camera back into his pocket. Typical of his Chinatown images is that of a butcher at work under the gaze of a young onlooker. Genthe could not pose his subjects, nor could he spend any time composing his photographs. Yet this picture, like many of his others, is marked not only by its dramatic content but by the expressive contrast of shadow and light that he was able to record. Adding to the power of the image is the look on the butcher's face suggesting that the man may well have spotted the elusive Genthe just as he was taking the picture.

The desire to capture images of vanishing or unique lifestyles was not confined to the United States. In France, for example, photographer Jacques-Henri Lartigue became a master of the straight documentary approach. Under any circumstances, the images that Lartigue captured during his long career would rank him as one of the masters of photography. What is almost impossible to believe is that he took some of

his greatest pictures between the time he was 10 and 12 years old.

When he was very young, Lartigue both adored and was jealous of his older brother Zissou, who was constantly experimenting with new contraptions and finding new adventures. In the diary that he kept throughout his life Lartigue would later write, "My brother Zissou had a vivid intelligence and he invented so many things . . . but I was always the little boy, in the way, kept in the corner, dying to take part." In 1903, when he was seven, Lartigue's frustrations were put to rest when his father gave him a camera so that he could record what he saw around him, particularly his brother's adventures. The camera was a huge contraption mounted on a tall tripod. Lartigue was so small that he had to stand on tiptoe on a stool to take his pictures. But he had found his life's purpose. In his diary he wrote, "Photography is a magic thing. Nothing will ever be as much fun."

Lartigue began his picture taking by capturing images of his large family at play, at home, at the seashore, and on vacation in the Normandy countryside. When he was 10, he acquired a hand-held camera and began taking some of his most memorable photographs. Many were of his brother and his friends as they experimented with kites and the earliest forms of airplanes. The prospect of the conquest of the air fascinated him and he constantly begged adults to take him to a nearby airfield, where he photographed pioneer pilots' continual attempts to fly. Before he was even a teenager, he compiled one of the earliest and most accurate records of the birth of flight.

Lartigue's fascination with machines extended to the automobile. Among his most compelling images are those of the automotive races at Orleans and Dieppe. He was also intrigued with the glamorous appearance of the elegantly dressed women of the day. The photographs he took of them on their daily morning walks or attending horseracing events constitute yet another photographic documentation of the era. The most distinguishing characteristics of his images were their total directness, clarity, and the sense of excitement they so often conveyed. For one so young, it was a remarkable achievement.

While Lartigue was capturing images of the romance and spirit of his times, another French photographer, Eugène Atget, was making his own vital photographic contribution. An orphan, Atget went to sea when he was very young, serving as a cabin boy. When his seafaring days were over, he spent more than 10 years trying to establish himself as a touring actor. Unable to earn enough money on the stage, at the age of 40 he decided to try his hand at photography. Needing to begin selling his photographs almost immediately, he found an outlet for his images in the large Parisian artists' colony. Many of these artists commonly purchased photographs of parks, gardens, buildings, and other scenes to use for visual reference for the paintings they created.

Eugène Atget. *St. Cloud,* about 1910.

A friend of Atget wrote about him, "For some time he had had the ambition to create a collection of all that which both in Paris and its surroundings was artistic and picturesque."

Eugène Atget. *Avenue des Gobleins, Paris,* about 1910.

Atget's storefront images rank among the most outstanding of all his photographs. Even though they are absent of people, there is an unmistakable human quality about them.

Brassaï (Gyula Halasz). Couple in café, about 1935.

"Most of the time I have drawn my images from the daily life around me. I think that is the most sincere and humble appreciation of reality, the most everyday event leads to the extraordinary," wrote Brassaï.

For more than a quarter century, from 1900 until 1927, Atget rose each day before dawn and roamed the streets of Paris taking his pictures. He chose the early hours when the streets would be almost empty so that he would be undisturbed by onlookers and so that he could spend as much time as he thought necessary to capture each image. A tireless worker, he took photographs of almost everything that met his eye. He captured the stores, the churches, the parks, the monuments, the courtyards, and the elegant specialty shops that gave Paris its distinctive flavor. He took many of his pictures in series, photographing workers of all types. He was particularly fascinated with the countless horsedrawn vehicles that dominated the Parisian streets. He photographed them all—coal, brewery, and laundry wagons, funeral coaches, milk and grocery carts.

There is a special poignancy to these images. All were taken at a time when Paris, like almost all major cities, was beginning to change dramatically in appearance. For one thing, miles of houses and shops

were being torn down to permit digging from the surface to build the Métro, the Paris subway system. Atget was aware that many of the finely detailed buildings he photographed would soon give way to more modern, less artistically adorned structures. He also knew that, because of the automobile, the horsedrawn vehicles would rapidly become part of the past. The photographs he took represent nothing less than a historical documentation of a vanishing Paris.

Atget's pictures of homes and buildings are marked by the attention he paid to every detail—railings, archways, doors, and staircases. Some of his most compelling photographs were those he took of the storefront windows of the many specialty shops for which Paris was famous. Typical of these is the image he captured of a men's clothing store. The dramatic play of the white signs against the dark clothing and the positions of the mannequins make it a dramatic image. It is a most human photograph, without any person appearing in it.

Atget's passion for documenting a great city before its appearance was dramatically altered in the name of progress was shared by the American photographer Berenice Abbott. As a member of a group of photographers who took their pictures under the auspices of the government's Works Progress Administration (WPA) during the Great Depression, Abbott compiled an unprecedented visual portrayal of New York City.

Abbott titled her photographic project *Changing New York.* To her, New York represented both "the present jostling with the past" and "life at its greatest intensity." She was determined to document as much of the city as possible before many of its buildings gave way to skyscrapers.

Abbott took hundreds of pictures from both street level and rooftops. Time and again she demonstrated a marvelous ability to capture striking contrasts of patterns, light, and shapes. Aware of the importance of her project she stated, "Photography can only represent the present. Once photographed, the subject becomes part of the past."

Among the documentary photographers were those who made their mark by recording what can best be described as the human condition. Their goal was to photographically capture people of all types as they made their way through life, documenting the joys and frustrations, the good and the not so good that are all part of the human experience. One of the giants of this approach was a man who gave himself the name Brassaï.

His real name was Gyula Halasz, but professionally he called himself Brassaï in honor of Brassov, Transylvania, the town in which he was born in 1899. When he was four years old, his father brought him to Paris and for the rest of his life he remained in love with that city. As a young man he studied art in both Hungary and Germany and then moved permanently to Paris, where he spent eight years working as a journalist. In 1929, encouraged by his friend the well-known photographer André Kertész, he took up photography.

The images that Brassaï captured from the time he turned to the camera can best

be described as slices of life. Unlike Eugène Atget, who photographed in the early morning hours, Brassaï preferred to work mostly at night. He felt that the atmosphere created by the evening light was most appropriate for capturing images of the various types of people he wished to photograph.

Brassaï was a highly intelligent man who gave great thought to every picture he took. He was a most deliberate photographer who would not snap his shutter until either the natural or artificial light falling upon his subjects and their expressions or

Berenice Abbott. *El, 1936.*

Abbott's Changing New York *series revealed her mastery at capturing the patterns formed by light and shadow. She took this picture from beneath one of New York City's many elevated railways.*

gestures were exactly as he wished. He used several different kinds of hand-held cameras, but his genius lay not in his use of his equipment but in his deep understanding of what it took to capture an outstanding documentary photograph.

The masterful documentary photographer, he wrote, "has respect for his subjects, amounting almost to religious veneration; keenness of powers of observation; patience and hawk-like speed on swooping on his prey; . . . spurning of color and the enjoyment derived form the restraint and sobriety of black upon white; and finally, desire to get beyond the anecdotal and to promote subjects to the dignity of types."

Brassaï's dedication to this vision made it possible for him to produce unique and

Tina Modotti—Photographer/Revolutionary/Spy

As in all areas of the creative arts, photography has had its share of interesting and even controversial characters. One of the most intriguing personalities of all was Tina Modotti, who took documentary and political-activist photographs in Mexico in the 1920s.

Born in Italy in 1896, Modotti came to San Francisco in 1913. Four years later she married a poet and artist, Roubaix Richey. In 1918 she became a movie actress, and during the next three years appeared in several Hollywood films. Just as her movie career was ending, her husband died and she became the companion of American photographer Edward Weston, who taught her photography.

In 1923 Modotti and Weston moved to Mexico, where they eventually opened two photographic studios. It was while she was in Mexico that Modotti's life changed even

more dramatically. She became friendly with some of Mexico's most active revolutionaries and joined the Communist Party. It was during this time also that she took her most outstanding photographs. Many were of various types of Mexican workers, whom she felt were being exploited by an oppressive government. Other pictures were images with a strong social-political message— revolutionary propaganda. Among the strongest such images were those in which she grouped together objects like an ear of corn, a guitar, a sickle, and a bandolier (a broad belt holding a long row of bullets) representing traditional Mexican ways of life contrasted with the struggle against oppression.

Modotti's revolutionary activities brought her to the attention of Mexican authorities. In 1928 she was accused of helping to murder a fellow revolu-

tionary with whom she had begun a romantic relationship. She was found innocent of that charge, but the following year was accused of taking part in an assassination attempt against Mexico's president and was deported. She first went to Germany, where she photographed for a magazine. She then went to live in Moscow, where she abandoned photography in favor of working full time for the Communist party.

From 1931 until 1934 Modotti worked for a Russian relief agency called International Red Aid. During that time she was also recruited by the Russian secret police and was sent on spying missions to several different countries. From 1935 to 1938 Modotti was in Spain, where during the Spanish Civil War she worked in a hospital and also supplied aid to orphans. In 1939 she returned to Mexico and was granted political asylum.

Three years later she died of a heart attack while riding in a taxi in Mexico City.

Throughout her lifetime Tina Modotti was known mainly for her political activities. In more recent times she has gained recognition for the quality and power of the social documentary images she captured in Mexico. Hers is a remarkable story, compiled by a woman whose life was as dramatic as the pictures she took.

Tina Modotti. Mexican workers' demonstration, 1929.

In keeping with her revolutionary beliefs, many of Modotti's photographs reveal the difficult life of Mexican laborers.

haunting photographs. "I invent nothing," he said, "I imagine everything."

The photographs taken by straight documentary photographers provided a great service to all those interested in preserving a record of the past and in gaining insight into the human condition. Thousands of images made their way into archives throughout the world where they are still studied by students, scholars, and the general public. Scores of books have included these visual records. It was, however, the images captured by social documentary photographers that had an even more direct impact. Building upon photography's ability to persuade as well as reveal, those who took social documentary photographs used their cameras to make people aware of conditions that they felt cried out for reform.

Many of these conditions involved people who lived in the city. By the middle of the 19th century, the movement from rural areas to cities was taking place in nations around the world. The cities were exciting places, filled with stores, restaurants, entertainment, and work opportunities of all kinds. For many, the city became a symbol of the progress that was being made throughout the globe. But there was a real price to this progress.

The factories that were located in most of the cities lured workers away from farming areas but paid very low wages. Most factory workers could not afford to live in clean, well-kept homes or neighborhoods. Newly arrived immigrants, most of whom were poor, also made up a large part of the urban population. One of the first to train his camera on city poor people and, in the process, produce pictures which showed conditions in

John Thomson. *London Nomades,* 1876.

There is a genuine similarity between many of Thomson's images and those of Frances Benjamin Johnston. Like Johnston, Thomson never demeaned any of his subjects in his photographs, even those, like these British gypsies, who were living on the edge of society.

need of reform was the British photographer John Thomson.

A passionate traveler, Thomson had journeyed to the Far East between 1865 and 1870, where he captured images of people and places few in the Western world had ever seen. Some of his most compelling photographs, however, were those he took of poor and destitute people living in harsh conditions in London. They were published in a book titled *Street Life in London* to accompany text written by the reform-minded reporter Adolphe Smith. The publication of Thomson's pictures represented a photographic breakthrough, since in Victorian England the depiction of the social problems of the "lower classes" was thought to be in bad taste. The impact that Thomson's pictures had on the public paved the way for other photographers who created even more shocking exposés of particular social ills connected with urban life. Of these, the photographer who

Jacob Riis. Woman and child in a tenement, about 1888.

This photograph of an Italian mother and her baby was typical of the thousands of pictures that Riis took inside New York City tenements. According to Riis, his purpose was to show "as no mere description could, the misery and vice that [I have] noticed . . . and suggest the direction in which good might be done."

succeeded in bringing about the most dramatic changes was the Danish-born Jacob Riis, who came to America at the age of 21. He lived in New York City at a time when millions of European immigrants in that metropolis were forced to live in terribly crowded, dirty, multistoried buildings called tenements.

Riis was primarily a reporter, not a photographer. But when he was assigned to write newspaper articles about the slums of New York he found that he needed to take photographs of the conditions he encountered so that people would believe his reports. He taught himself how to take pictures and, beginning in 1877, took his camera into the tenements and on to the streets and alleys where the immigrants continually sought refuge from their crowded, shabby dwellings. The faces of the people he photographed reflected the pain and bewilderment of the life they were forced to endure.

Riis made a concerted effort to portray his subjects in as dignified a manner as possible. Despite this, he often encountered bitter resistance to his picture taking. Many tenement dwellers, embarrassed or angry at being photographed in such squalid surroundings, resisted his photographic attempts. On several occasions he was driven from a dwelling by threats to his person or by a barrage of thrown objects.

But he was not to be deterred. For several years he continued to compile a dramatic visual record of those in desperate need of help. Among the most telling of Riis's photographs is his picture of a woman holding her baby in the basement of a tenement. The horrible living conditions, the sparse belongings and the sense of hopelessness, as reflected in the woman's expression, are all revealed.

Riis's images were widely circulated. Many were published in newspapers and in books with such titles as *How the Other Half*

Lives (1890) and *Children of the Tenements,* (1892). They shocked the nation, but most important, they inspired city and national government officials to begin to take steps to eliminate the conditions under which so many newcomers to America had been forced to live.

Lewis Hine was another photographer endowed with a deep social conscience. Trained as both a sociologist and a teacher, Hine took his first photographs at the age of 37 when he was hired to teach social science and to take publicity pictures for a private school. Increasingly fascinated with what he could do through his new-found photography, he started taking pictures of various aspects of New York working-class life, many of which he used as teaching tools in his social science classes.

Like Jacob Riis, Hine was concerned with the plight of the thousands of immigrants who were arriving daily in New York. One of the first series of pictures he took was of newcomers moments after they first set foot on American soil at the immigration depot at New York's Ellis Island. Inspired by the results of these images, Hine signed on as a staff photographer for a magazine.

The photographs he took for the publication caught the attention of the National Child Labor Committee which, in 1908, hired him to document photographically what had become a national disgrace. Nearly 2 million children, aged six to 14, worked for pennies a day in the nation's factories, mines, canneries, quarries, and on the streets. They had no time for schooling and worked under the most difficult conditions.

In order to compile his photographic documentation, Hine traveled extensively. He journeyed to the coalfields of Pennsylvania, where in mines deep beneath the earth he photographed boys as young as 10 years old bent over for hours in awkward

Jack Delano. Farm couple, 1940.

Many of the Farm Security Administration (FSA) photographers provided visual testimony to the indomitable spirit of people caught up in the worst of times. Dorothea Lange spoke for all her fellow FSA photographers when she stated: "I had to get my camera to register the things about these people that were more important than how poor they were—their pride, their strength, their spirit."

positions sorting coal (see page 74). He took his camera to California, where he captured images of children standing all day on wet, cold floors shucking oysters, often working with fingers sliced by the sharp-edged shells or the shucking knife. Many of his most dramatic photographs were those he took in the factories of New England and the South where boys and girls worked from dawn to dusk operating immense, highly dangerous machines.

When Hine's long and arduous documentation was completed, the National Child Labor Committee presented his images to Congress. They were also widely published in newspapers and magazines. Like the pictures of the slums that Jacob Riis had produced before him, Lewis

Hine's child labor photographs stirred the emotions of the nation. Due in great measure to the evidence he captured with his camera, the first national child labor laws were enacted.

Most documentary photographers either worked independently or for publications. In the 1930s and early 1940s, however, a group of 10 men and two women made their mark as documentarians by making an enormous photographic record of work done by the Farm Security Administration (FSA), a United States government agricultural relief agency. Collectively, the some 270,000 photographs they produced represent what is widely regarded as the most powerful single collection of images ever compiled. As far as documentary photography is concerned, the Farm Security Administration collection is unique in another way as well. For within this massive compilation are both outstanding straight documentary photographs and compelling social documentary images.

The FSA photographic project came about as a result of the most severe economic depression the United States had ever experienced. As the stock market collapsed, millions of people, beginning in the early 1930s, found themselves out of work. One part of the nation was particularly hard hit. Farmers in both the Southeast and the Southwest suffered from the economic collapse that drastically forced down the prices people could pay for food. In addition, those in the Southwest had experienced years of drought that had turned their soil into dust. Tens of thousands, having lost their farms, took to the road, heading

Dorothea Lange. Migrants, 1935.

Lange was always aware of the impact that her photographs of displaced farm families would have on the viewing public. "The camera," she stated, "is an instrument that teaches people how to see without a camera."

Marion Post Wolcott. Segregated movie theatre, 1939.

Although she has never received the acclaim given to Dorothea Lange and Walker Evans, Wolcott was one of the most talented and effective of the FSA photographers. This photograph not only reveals the deep racial prejudice that was part of the American scene in the 1930s but also stands on its own as a beautifully composed image.

for California, Oregon, and Washington State in search of agricultural jobs.

In Washington, D.C., President Franklin D. Roosevelt established the Farm Security Administration, designed to bring relief to the hard-pressed farmers. The agency, in turn, created an Historical Section, one of whose major tasks was to document photographically the help that the FSA would be giving to those it was set up to serve. Roy Stryker, a Columbia University professor known for his understanding of photography's value in making records as well as for his organizational skills, was chosen to direct the Historical Section. He began by hiring some of the nation's most socially committed photographers to capture the images. Among them were Dorothea Lange, Walker Evans, Russell Lee, Arthur Rothstein, Jack Delano, and Marion Post Wolcott.

Stryker was a man who knew how to seize an opportunity. He was aware that his photographers needed to capture images of FSA agents helping people cope with their desperate situation. That, after all, was the stated purpose of the Historical Section. But he realized also that such an array of photographic talent, combined with government support and funding, presented the unique opportunity to capture nothing less than a portrayal of a people and a nation.

When Stryker gave his orders to his photographers he directed them not only to document the hard times that so many people were undergoing, but to capture images of rural people and agricultural workers of all types engaged in their daily activities. His goal, he stated, was to introduce America to Americans. The FSA photographers responded by producing tens of thousands of documentary pictures chronicling almost every aspect of the people whose lives were most devastated by the Great Depression.

Two of the FSA photographers in particular, Dorothea Lange and Walker Evans, earned fame through the pictures they took for the agency. Lange became known for the sensitivity she brought to each of her images. She was able, better than any other FSA photographer, to gain the confidence of her subjects and to produce pictures that directly connect the viewer with both the humanity and the emotions of people undergoing desperate hardship.

Walker Evans established himself as a photographic giant through the supremely narrative quality of his work. In documenting the plight of hard-hit southern farmers Evans produced pictures that told more about their condition, their possessions, the towns they frequented than pages of text could ever achieve. Many of his photographs spoke eloquently about people and their way of life through a portrayal of their daily artifacts. As one photohistorian stated, "Usually Mr. Evans has dismissed the dweller from his dwelling, but we can deduce him."

Walker Evans.
Country store, 1936.

Signs, calendars, everyday objects and products— these were all ingredients of many of Evans's most compelling photographs. Evans's Let Us Now Praise Famous Men, *compiled with author James Agee, remains one of the most important photographic books ever published.*

Paul Conklin. Young Appalachian woman, 1965.

The United States Office of Economic Opportunity (OEO) project not only produced memorable and moving images but also gave its young photographers the opportunity to develop their skills fully. As such it provided another example of the vital role that government has sometimes played in furthering the advancement of photography.

One of the most well known of Evans's images is his photograph of the interior of a country store. Distinguished by Evans' ability to contrast light and shade and his highly developed sense of composition, it is reminiscent of Eugène Atget's storefront images. For it too speaks eloquently about people and their way of life without containing a single human being.

It is almost impossible to overstate the importance of the FSA photographs to photography in general and to documentary photography in particular. More than 60 years after most of them were taken, the evaluation of them made by photographer Edward Steichen still rings true. They are, he stated, "the most remarkable human documents that were ever rendered in pictures."

One of the major contributions of the FSA photographers was the way in which, through their work, they set a standard for all documentary photographers who would follow. In the 1960s, for example, another government-sponsored collection of photographs portraying people caught up in difficult circumstances was compiled.

These images were captured by photographers hired by the United States Office of Economic Opportunity (OEO). Included among these photographers were such talented cameramen and women as William Warren; Linda Bartlett; Arthur Tress, who later established himself as among the most innovative of modern photographers; and Marcia Keegan, arguably the most accomplished of all of today's photographers of Native Americans of the Southwest.

The people that the OEO photographers recorded were among the millions who dwelled in what some sociologists termed "the other America," individuals who, while living in one of the richest nations in the world, found themselves on the edge of poverty. Unlike the FSA images, however, the OEO photographs have remained almost unknown. Like images captured by all those who mastered the documentary approach, they make us aware that the most outstanding photographs are those that not only appeal to the eye but touch deeply the emotions of the viewer as well.

21. Juli 1929
Nummer 29
38. Jahrgang

Berliner

Preis
des Heftes
20 Pfennig

Illustrirte Zeitung

Verlag Ullstein

Berlin SW 68

Aufnahme Munkacsi.

Ferienfreude.

Chapter Six

Photographs in Print

The history of photography has been characterized by a continual series of technical advancements that have made picture taking easier and have made photographs more accessible to the worldwide public. Among the most important of these advances was the halftone printing process, introduced in the 1880s. This technique made it possible to publish photographs alongside words on the printed page. It was a breakthrough that led the photograph to become one of the chief means by which people around the world get their news and form their opinions about world events.

Nonphotographic illustrations had appeared in newspapers, magazines, and books since the late 1830s. The first weekly publication to use illustrations extensively was the *Illustrated London News* in 1842. Its immediate success led to the establishment of similar publications around the world. Included in these picture weeklies were *L'Illustration* in France, *L'Illustrazione* in Italy, *Revista Universale* in Mexico, *A Illustracato* in Brazil, the *Illustrated Australian News,* and *Harper's Weekly* and *Frank Leslie's Illustrated Newspaper* in the United States.

Almost all the illustrations in these early publications were wood engravings made by technicians who, with their sharp cutting tools, traced the lines of a sketch, drawing, or photograph that had been placed on a block of wood by a draftsman. They removed the unneeded wood, leaving the lines of the picture in raised relief. Ink was then applied and paper was pressed against the block, transferring the image to it, similar to using a rubber stamp.

All this changed with the perfection of halftone reproduction of pictures. Many individuals had worked toward making the process a reality but major credit for its full development is given to the inventors Frederic Ives, Stephen Horgan, and Max Levy in the United States and George Meissenbach in Germany.

The key to the halftone process is to break up the continuous tones of a photograph into a pattern of dots that are essentially unnoticeable to the eye. This is done by making a copy photograph of the original with a rectangular mesh of fine lines—somewhat like a window screen—in front of the film. The intersecting lines on the screen break the image into a regularly

The invention that allowed photographs to be published alongside text led to the birth of photographic magazines. One of the earliest was Germany's Berliner Illustrierte Zeitung (Berlin Illustrated Newspaper).

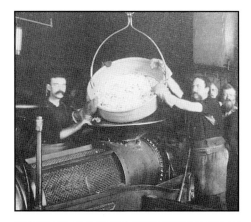

Frances Benjamin Johnston.
Whitening Process, about 1900.

Photographs were used as a basis for magazine and book illustrations well before the halftone printing process was invented. Illustrators would use a photograph as the model for a woodcut that copied the scene in the photograph as closely as possible. Johnston's photograph (top) of one step in the process of pressing coins appeared as a woodcut (bottom) in a popular magazine of the time.

spaced pattern of dots that are large in dark-tone areas of the picture being reproduced, smaller in middle-tone areas, and tiny in the lightest areas. The resulting negative is used to make a printing plate with a corresponding pattern of raised dots that receive the ink. When a print is made, the black ink transferred from the largest dots runs together, or nearly so, in the darkest areas. In the middle tones, more paper shows between the smaller dots and the eye blends the amounts of black and white it sees to form the impression of various gray tones. In the highlights, the very tiny dots are almost invisible; the eye sees mostly white paper and gets the impression of very light grays and white.

In modern printing, a halftone screen is no longer used. Instead, the dot pattern is produced by scanning the original picture at high speed with a laser beam. The light reflected from the print or transmitted through a slide is electronically sampled several hundred times a second. The individual samples, called *pixels* (short for "picture elements") correspond to dots. They are recorded digitally by computer circuitry and used to control the intensity of another laser that exposes a printing plate.

The halftone process dramatically changed the nature of newspapers and magazines. By the early 1900s, photographs began to appear regularly in many publications. In the process, new forms of photography and a whole new category of photographers, known generally as press photographers, were created.

From its beginnings, press photography has fallen into two basic categories: news photography and photojournalism. News

photographs are those that depict events of importance or interest at the time they take place or immediately afterward. Photojournalism is that form of photography in which pictures, usually in a series, are used as the main vehicle for telling a story. Series of this type usually appear in magazines.

The rapid growth and popularity of these new forms of picture taking created broad opportunities for photographers. Along with these opportunities came many new challenges, particularly for news photographers. For what those who entered this field quickly discovered was that there were special skills required in capturing effective images of newsworthy events. Among these were the ability to anticipate when such an event was about to take place, the talent to snap pictures at the exact moment the event was happening, and the stamina to be constantly on the move to fulfill photographic news assignments.

In meeting these challenges, photographers were aided immeasurably by significant technological advancements that took place as news photography and later photojournalism became increasingly popular. Primary among these advances was the development of 35mm cameras, fast film, electronic flash equipment, and a variety of sophisticated lenses.

The camera that had the greatest impact on press photography was the Leica. It was invented in Germany in 1913 by Oscar Barnack and was marketed, beginning in 1925, by the German optical company E. Leitz Optische Werke. The Leica, which used 35mm film, was light and easy to handle and permitted taking 36 pictures before having to be reloaded.

The immediate success of the Leica led to the development of other cameras suitable for photojournalism, most notably the twin-lens Rolleiflex introduced in 1930, which used 120 size roll film. The work of press photographers was also made more effective by the development of small flashbulbs and associated equipment such as the Burvin Synchronizer, specifically designed to mount on small cameras like the Leica for on-the-spot flash lighting.

Two other technological advancements also had a significant effect on the growth of press photography. One was the development, soon after the halftone was introduced, of *rotogravure,* an adaptation of the photogravure process invented by Karl Klic in 1879. The other was the invention of wire and radio transmission of images.

The halftone process prints the same density of ink for every dot, whatever its size. The photogravure process creates pits, rather than raised dots, to hold ink on the printing plate. The pits are all the same size, but of different depths, so they hold various amounts of ink. Therefore, the darkness or lightness of a printed tone depends on how dense the ink is at each point. This is almost the same as in the original photograph, where tones are created by different densities of developed silver. Photogravure reproductions can look almost like photographs themselves. The process was used by many art photographers such as Peter Henry Emerson in the late 19th century. However, it was impractical for newspaper and magazine printing, because it was expensive and time consuming to prepare a plate and produced only a few thousand reproductions before the plate had to be replaced. Rotogravure, also developed by Klic, in 1890, overcame these problems. It produced gravure plates for printing pictures and text simultaneously that were mounted on the large-diameter cylinders of high-speed rotary presses. One of the first weekly rotogravure newspaper sections appeared in England in 1912. By the 1920s newspapers around the world included a rotogravure section made up almost entirely of photographs in their Sunday editions.

In the late 1920s, press photography was greatly advanced by the perfection of an electronic system that permitted photographs to be transmitted by wire or cable and later by radio. Using this system, a photographic news service in America, for example, inserted a photograph into a machine that was the forerunner of today's fax machines and computer scanners. The machine directed a narrow beam of light in a series of lines across the picture and generated a varying electrical signal from the reflected light. The signal was transmitted to a recipient in the United States or overseas, where a receiving machine generated a copy of it.

The speed with which photographs could now be sent from field bureaus to a newspaper's headquarters for printing in the next edition was a giant step forward in bringing newsworthy images to the public as quickly as possible. It also accelerated the establishment of photographic departments within agencies such as the Associated Press and United Press International, to supply news photographs as well as written news reports to publications throughout the world.

News photographers were greatly aided in meeting the demands of their work by the development of new lighter and faster cameras. The German Leica (top) and the Japanese Kwanon (bottom, later changed to Canon) in these advertisements from about 1930 were two of the most widely used.

Eddie Adams. General shoots
Viet Cong prisoner, 1968.

*When he took this picture, Adams
had no idea of the impact it would
have or the fame that this single
image would bring him. Within a
year, the photograph was awarded
the Pulitzer Prize and took first
prize in almost every news photograph contest throughout the world.*

Captain Cecil W. Stoughton.
Lyndon B. Johnson taking oath as
President, 1963.

*This photograph, taken shortly after
President John F. Kennedy was assassinated, was printed in newspapers
throughout the world. Vice President
Lyndon B. Johnson is being sworn in
as President while a devastated Mrs.
Kennedy looks on.*

All these many advancements in equipment, printing methods, and distribution,
combined with the skills of individual news
photographers, led to some of the most
unforgettable photographs ever taken. Pictures such as that of Charles Lindbergh
landing in Paris after completing the first
solo flight across the Atlantic in 1927, of the
sudden fiery explosion of the German diri-
gible "Hindenburg" in 1937, of the raising
of the American flag on the island of Iwo
Jima in 1945 after two months of brutal
World War II fighting, of Dr. Martin Luther
King, Jr., delivering his "I Have a Dream"
speech in 1963, to name but a few, have
demonstrated the power and the lasting
effect of the news photograph.

Some news photographs have had such
influence that they have profoundly affected public opinion and changed the course
of events. Such a picture was that taken
during the Vietnam War by Associated Press
cameraman Eddie Adams. In January 1968,
North Vietnamese troops invaded South
Vietnam. On February 1, some of these
troops infiltrated Saigon, South Vietnam's
capital city. Informed of what was taking
place in the city, Adams rushed to the site.
As he arrived, he encountered a horrifying
sight. A South Vietnamese officer stood
with his pistol pointed at the head of one
of the North Vietnamese infiltrators. Adams
quickly snapped a picture only seconds
before the officer fired and killed the man.

Adams's photograph was developed in
the Associated Press Saigon office and
transmitted around the world. Outraged
viewers flooded Associated Press offices
with telegrams. The impact of the photograph was greatest in the United States, a
country torn apart by bitter disagree-
ments over its participation in the war.

The picture fueled efforts of those who opposed the conflict and changed the minds of a significant number of those who supported it.

The vast majority of news photographs have been taken by little-known photographers. There have, however, been some men and women who, through the body of work they produced, established themselves as masters of this photographic approach. Among the earliest was Jesse Tarbox Beals.

As a young photographer Beals had been both a portraitist and a traveling camera-woman. In 1902, impressed by her work, the Buffalo *Courier* hired her to head its newly formed photographic department. In 1903 she achieved what was probably the nation's first news photography scoop when she covered a murder trial. Upon arriving at the courtroom she found that the judge had refused to allow pictures to be taken of the proceedings. Demonstrating the perseverance that would mark legions of news photographers to follow, Beals placed a chair next to the courtroom door, on the outside. She then climbed up on it and took the only pictures of the trial by shooting through the transom above the door.

Many of the images that Beals captured were taken in New York City's tenement districts. As seen in her photograph of a father and his three children, she had a way of putting children at ease and getting them to pose for her. As in many of her tenement pictures, Beals positioned one youngster in the foreground of the image and placed the father and the other two children in a room at the rear, framed by a doorway. The result was a picture that was three-dimensional in effect. Beals's tenement images were published in many newspapers.

Like the pictures taken by Jacob Riis, they helped inspire government officials to take action to clean up the slums.

While Jesse Tarbox Beals took news photographs of almost every type of happening or situation, another photographer made his greatest impact by training his camera on a particular type of subject. A Polish immigrant to America, his name was Usher Fellig. When, in the early 1930s, he went to work as photographer for several New York newspapers he adopted the name Weegee.

In the 1930s and '40s, mob wars and murders carried out by crime syndicates became commonplace in New York. It was the kind of subject that attracted many readers to the newspapers for which Weegee worked. He became a master at photographing mobster activities and crime scenes. Typical of these images is the

Jesse Tarbox Beals. Family in tenement, about 1905.

Beals was one of the most prolific of all the early news photographers. This photograph is one of the many she took to accompany articles describing the wretched conditions of the New York City tenement district.

Weegee (Usher "Arthur" Fellig). *Their First Murder*, 1941.

Weegee's greatest talent was his ability to capture the various emotions registered in the faces of those he photographed. "Many photographers live in a dream world of beautiful backgrounds," he wrote. "It wouldn't hurt them to get a taste of reality to wake them up."

picture he took of a group of people newly arrived at the scene of a murder. The photograph is marked by Weegee's special ability to capture the full range of human emotions. The girl in the left foreground appears stunned. The woman in the center of the picture is obviously in anguish. Others seem stunned or curious, while the young man at the far left, for whatever reason, sports a broad smile.

Personally, Weegee was a most outrageous man. Early on, for example, he found that he had problems photographing mobsters in their limousines. This was because most of their activities were at night and the black limousines did not show up as well as he would have liked in his photographs. He actually had the audacity to contact some well-known mob bosses and ask them if they would switch to lighter-colored vehicles so he could photograph them better. Although they refused, his suggestion provided an example of how far he would go in an attempt to get the pictures he desired. Always a self-promoter, he stamped the back of each of his photographs with the statement, "Credit Weegee the Famous."

By the end of the 1920s, photographs in newspapers had become one of the world's most common forms of communi-

cation. Aware of their readers' increasing dependence upon pictures to get their news, various newspaper publishers took a bold step. Rather than printing only a single picture that illustrated a newsworthy event, they began including groups of photographs which, in themselves, told a story or gave readers deeper insights into a particular subject.

This movement toward the picture story was most fully launched in Germany. There, newspapers such as the *Berliner Illustrierte Zeitung* (Berlin Illustrated Newspaper), the *Müchener Illustrierte Presse* (Munich Illustrated Press), and the *Arbeiter Illustrierte Zeitung* (Worker's Illustrated Newspaper) increasingly filled their pages with stories told through photographs.

This approach became so popular that soon magazines in which picture stories dominated the pages were established. These early photograph-oriented publications included *Picture Post* in England, *Vu* and *Paris Match* in France, and *Colliers, Fortune,* and *National Geographic* in the United States. Out of these new picture magazines grew both photojournalism and the photo essay.

Like the newspaper photographers who faced special challenges in capturing events as they took place, the men and women who became photojournalists were required to possess special skills in order to compile their photographic stories, or photo essays, as they came to be called. An effective photojournalist had to be able to conceive a story that would be of significant interest to viewers, had to plan what types of photographs would best convey that story, and had to have the ability to capture a sequence of images that would best move the story along from beginning to end.

Many photojournalists were able to meet these challenges so well that they produced photo essays that touched deeply on the emotions of most who viewed them. Contained within some of these picture stories were individual photographs which have remained etched in the public memory.

Many of the photographers destined to become masters of photojournalism were either employed by or worked on special assignment for a magazine called *Life*. Launched in 1936 by Henry Luce, who had previously founded *Time*, a news magazine that used comparatively few pictures, and *Fortune*, a business magazine that featured many photographs, *Life* became the most widely read magazine of its day. It brought photographs into the homes of millions of people throughout the globe and established the photo essay as one of the principal means of conveying human conditions and world developments. The enormous scope of the magazine could be seen in its stated purpose. "To see life, to see the world; to eyewitness great events; to watch the faces of the poor and the gestures of the proud"; *Life*'s editors wrote, "to see strange things; . . . to see man's work; . . . to see and take pleasure in seeing; to see and be amazed; to see and be instructed."

Many of the photo essays created by *Life* photographers remain among the most powerful ever compiled. Some touched *Life*'s readers so deeply that many of these readers became personally involved with the subjects of the picture stories. In 1961, for example, *Life* published Gordon Parks's picture story of a 12-year-old boy named Flavio da Silva who, with his poverty-stricken parents and their eight other children, lived in a slum in the hills outside Rio

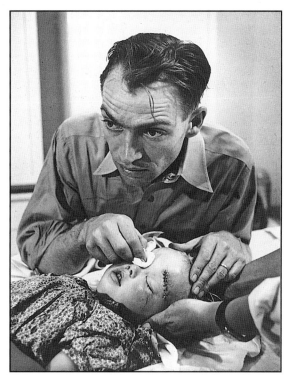

W. Eugene Smith. Photograph from "Country Doctor" photo essay, 1945.

Smith was one of the most talented of all the photo essayists. This picture is from a photo essay he created for Life *magazine depicting a day in the life of a country doctor. The doctor is seen stitching up a cut on a child's forehead, just one of many medical tasks he completed in a single day as Smith followed him with his camera.*

de Janeiro in Brazil. Flavio suffered from severe asthma attacks. Parks's pictures of his suffering, of his parents and his brothers and sisters sleeping in one bed, and of the horrendous conditions in general in which the family lived elicited a huge emotional response from *Life*'s readers. Letters poured into the magazine's offices. Many contained money, which *Life* gave to Flavio and his family. Some letters included offers to adopt the boy. Thanks to the power of Parks's photographs, the Children's Asthma Research Institute and Hospital in Denver arranged for Flavio to be brought to its facilities, where he was treated for his asthmatic condition free of charge.

Through the images they captured, several *Life* photographers became internationally known. One, Margaret Bourke-White, became one of the most famous

A skier flies through the air over Innsbruck, Austria, in the 1957 International Ski Jumping Contest. The ability to print photographs alongside text led to the birth of sports photography. Pictures of athletic events and achievements became so popular that it was not long before magazines devoted entirely to sports made their appearance.

photographers in the world. Raised in Bound Brook, New Jersey, Bourke-White attended seven colleges before finally earning a degree from Cornell University. Her life changed dramatically when, in the early 1920s, she discovered photography. "We all find something," she would later write, "that is just right for us, and after I found the camera I never really felt a whole person again unless I was planning pictures or taking them."

The cover of *Life*'s very first issue featured a Bourke-White photograph. The main story in the initial issue was a photo essay taken by her. For the next 21 years, she was one of *Life*'s most prolific photographers. She took pictures in almost every corner of the globe. She photographed miners in South Africa, wealthy landowners in Hungary, and peasants throughout Europe. She was the only non-Russian allowed to photograph the bombing of Moscow by the Germans in World War II. In 1943, she became the first woman photographer to fly on a United States combat mission.

The many assignments carried out by *Life*'s photographers and by all the photo-journalists who worked for countless other picture magazines frequently placed them in difficult and often dangerous situations. In Europe, for example, the French photographer Henri Cartier-Bresson captured many of his images at a time marked both by the prospect of war and a bitter conflict itself. Cartier-Bresson was a man who had no doubts as to what constituted the vital element in capturing a compelling photojournalistic image. "Photography," he stated, "is for me . . . based on the pleasure of observing and the ability to capture a decisive moment in a constant struggle with time." Over a long career, Cartier-Bresson captured hundreds of such "decisive moments." In any situation, emotions, facial expressions, and movements are always shifting and changing, he explained. This creates a stream of instants when these things come together and make the meaning or feeling of the situation visually clear. Then that instant is gone, but others will follow. These are the decisive moments when pictures should be taken. Photohistorian Beaumont Newhall noted the photographer's uncanny ability to capture such

Advertising and Fashion Photography

The ability to print photographs in magazines had a dramatic effect on the world of advertising. Manufacturers could now use photos in their ads which, in most cases, were far more effective as a selling tool than drawings. While many areas of business increasingly turned to photographs to entice customers to buy their goods, the greatest impact was felt in the fashion industry. For clothing designers and merchants, fashion photography presented the greatest vehicle they had ever had for introducing new clothing trends and selling their merchandise. Just as *Life* had introduced people everywhere to photojournalism and *Fortune* had promoted the industrial photograph, magazines like *Vogue, Vanity Fair, Harper's Bazaar,* and *Women's Home Companion* helped turn fashion photography into an art all its own.

Art et Decoration, in Paris, and *Vogue* were the two magazines that pioneered the fashion image. As early as 1913, *Vogue* began to feature the photographs of Adolf de Meyer, the man who is now commonly regarded as the world's first great fashion photographer. De Meyer's work was characterized by his ability to capture the textures in the clothing worn by his subjects in images that were tonally rich and dazzling with light.

Edward Steichen's photographs of the latest styles appeared in *Art et Decoration* in 1911, and by the beginning of the 1920s *Vogue* was featuring his fashion images. Steichen

brought a new look to the then still-infant world of fashion photography in the way he composed his pictures. He arranged his models into several groups and placed these groups at various places within the camera's eye. This gave a dramatic sense of design to the photographs, making them arresting images in their own right. His photographic style changed to keep up with the styles of the times, and he soon surpassed De Meyer, who seemed less adaptable.

In the 1930s, American photographer Toni Frissell pioneered another important approach to fashion photography. Frissell was the first to take models away from the confines of the studio and to photograph them in exotic places around the world. These dramatic settings and the animated poses she created for her models resulted in a whole new type of fashion image. Frissell's techniques were soon copied by fashion photographers throughout the world.

By the 1950s, fashion photography had become one of the most commonly encountered forms of the medium. Then and in the decades that followed, two photographers in particular, Irving Penn and Richard Avedon, elevated the fashion image to new heights. Working with the simplest lighting and without special props, Penn created pictures that captured viewers' attention through bold contrasts and poses that emphasized the almost abstract forms of the garments. In other pictures he created striking still-life arrangements of jewelry, gloves, and purses, and other accessories. He pio-

Toni Frissell. *Tyrall Plantation, Jamaica,* 1948.
Frissell changed the world of fashion photography by photographing her models in intriguing outdoor settings. It was a technique that soon became standard practice for fashion photographers.

neered big, bold closeups of lips and eyes to show new lipstick colors, eye shadow, and other cosmetics.

Richard Avedon's approach was, in many ways, the opposite of that taken by Irving Penn. His fashion pictures had an air of energetic, unrehearsed elegance and sophistication about them. Many of Avedon's techniques, including his use of electronic flash to dramatically freeze movement in mid-phase, have been copied by today's fashion photographers.

In more recent times, certain photographers have set new standards in fashion photography through the dramatic and colorful images they have captured

as part of ongoing advertising campaigns for specific clients. American Bruce Weber, for example, has become known for the consistently imaginative photographs he has taken for such clients as Ralph Lauren, Calvin Klein, and Banana Republic, and which have appeared in *GQ, Details, Vogue,* and other fashion magazines.

In the l980s and '90s, many of these publications increasingly adopted the practice of using celebrities, particularly movie and television stars and noted sports figures, as models for the clothing they featured. The British photographer David Bailey has been among the most prolific of

those who have focused on capturing the lifestyles of the famous while featuring their often trend-setting choices in fashions.

Perhaps the best known of today's photographers who have helped turn fashion photography into an art form is the American Annie Leibowitz. One of the most admired portrait photographers, Leibowitz has become recognized as well for her advertising images. She won particular acclaim for the compelling photographs she took for her advertising campaigns on behalf of American Express and The Gap. Her fashion images continue to appear regularly in *Vanity Fair* and *Vogue.*

Henri Cartier-Bresson. Children playing among ruins, Spain, 1933.

"Of all the means of expression," wrote Cartier-Bresson, "photography is the only one that fixes forever the precise and transitory instant. We photographers deal in things which are continually vanishing, and when they have vanished, there is no contrivance on earth which can make them come back again. We cannot develop and print a memory."

moments: "Cartier-Bresson is able to seize the split second when the subject stands revealed in its most significant aspect and most evocative form."

Cartier-Bresson began photographing seriously after encountering a series of Eugène Atget's photographs. For nine years, beginning in 1931, he photographed throughout Europe, demonstrating an openness to the world that would characterize all his work. In 1940, however, a year after World War II broke out, he was drafted into the French army. Captured by the Germans, he spent three years in a prisoner-of-war camp. After three separate attempts, he managed to escape from the prison camp and spent the rest of the war working in the French resistance movement.

When the war was finally over, Cartier-Bresson resumed his photographic career, carrying out assignments all over the world. Unlike photojournalists who pursued the physical action of events and the important people involved, Cartier-Bresson most often showed how the events affected ordinary people, how they reacted and responded. Among his subjects were Portuguese fishermen, villagers in Romania, Yugoslavia, and Greece, refugees in India and Pakistan, European residents in China when the change to Communism

occurred, pedestrians in Italy and Russia, and picnickers along rivers in France. His subjects were in many ways the same kind of people as the magazine readers who would see the pictures. This "everyday," human quality of his photographs gave them immense appeal. Some of his most powerful images were those he took of children in war-torn Europe. His picture of youngsters playing in bombed-out ruins during the Spanish Civil War of 1936–39 stands out as one of his very best. By capturing the youngster in the right foreground just as he was climbing on some debris and picturing the young man in the background just as he was about to throw a stone, Cartier-Bresson provides evidence of what he meant by "the decisive moment." His use of the huge hole in the wall to frame the picture and the positioning of the other children in the image reveals the way in which almost all his photographs were masterfully composed.

Margaret Bourke-White and Henri Cartier-Bresson set a standard for all future photojournalists through the ways in which they demonstrated their determination to capture the images they sought no matter how great the challenges. Beginning in the 1950s, a group of African photographers followed in this tradition by demonstrating their willingness to take enormous chances in order to take pictures they felt the world needed to see. These photographers worked for the South African magazine *Drum*. They continually risked their lives in order to capture images portraying the evils of apartheid (the name of the policy of racial segregation in South Africa).

In presenting photographs of apartheid and of black Africans' struggle for freedom,

Peter Magubane. Couple dancing, 1957.

Although Magubane devoted most of his photographic career to depicting black South Africans' struggle for freedom, he also photographed other subjects. Like many of his images, this picture appeared in Drum *magazine.*

Drum's owner, Jim Bailey, and editor Anthony Sampson accomplished what can be regarded as a publication miracle. Although many South African magazines had been banned after printing such pictures, Bailey and Sampson somehow managed to include anti-apartheid photographs in *Drum* along with pictures of weddings, nightlife, and other events.

The photographers who contributed to *Drum* were a talented and courageous lot. In order to create their picture stories they often donned disguises to get into places from which they otherwise would have been kept out. Some, determined to take pictures inside South Africa's notorious prisons, actually got themselves arrested and took hidden cameras inside their cells. Typical of these photojournalists was the South African photographer Peter Magubane. In 1969 while he was taking pictures for *Drum* and for a daily newspaper, Magubane was arrested for supposed crimes against the state. After two years in prison he was released, but he was banned from taking photographs for five years.

When the five years were over Magubane resumed his photojournalistic career. Undaunted by continual government scrutiny, he continued to take photographs of apartheid practices, particularly the exploitation of black African children. Late in his career Magubane spoke for many of his fellow African photographers when he stated, "In my work, and in the kind of pictures I chose to produce, I wanted to liberate myself, liberate my people, liberate the oppressor and let the world understand through my images what we were going through, what apartheid meant . . . to capture the images

that would make the world understand why black people are so angry in this country of South Africa. I said to myself, 'I don't care. If I die for the cause, so be it. If I see a picture . . . at all costs, I will try to get that picture.'"

The vast majority of photographs that appeared in *Life, Drum,* and the other news magazines were of people. There was, however, another type of subject which, beginning in the 1930s, increasingly captured photographic attention. The picture magazines had come into being at a time when, after decades of industrial development, machines and huge structures allied to industrialism increasingly dotted the landscape. For many people around the world these machines and structures, such as manufacturing plants, bridges, and dams, became powerful symbols, not only of the progress that had been made but of even greater advancements that seemed to lie ahead. Aware of the fascination with the icons of industrialism, those who published

Margaret Bourke-White. *Ammonia Gas Tanks*, 1938.

Bourke-White's appreciation of the beauty created by the lines of industrial structures can be seen in this picture of giant storage tanks. Along with photographing industrial objects in their entirety, Bourke-White, like many other industrial photographers, often focused her camera on details within massive structures and machinery.

Charles Sheeler. *Ford Plant, Detroit*, 1927.

For many years, Sheeler's photographs, like this image of an automobile plant outside of Detroit, Michigan, were far less heralded than his paintings. Today they have come to be recognized as equally powerful representations of his unique vision.

the picture magazines made certain that many of their issues contained pictures of the latest machines and structures. Out of this emerged yet another photographic approach known as industrial photography.

While those who took up this approach came from many nations, two American photographers in particular, Margaret Bourke-White and Charles Sheeler, produced some of the most compelling of all industrial images. Bourke-White and Sheeler shared a common motivation for taking their industrial photographs. Aside from the symbolic nature of the machinery and structures they wished to portray, both found a very special beauty in industrial objects. It was this vision that led to the special quality of their images.

Before becoming a major *Life* photographer, Bourke-White had taken many industrial photographs for *Fortune*. It was *Fortune* that championed industrial photography, much in the same manner as *Life* promoted and inspired photojournalism. The photographs that Bourke-White took for *Fortune,* as well as the many other industrial images she captured, were characterized by the way she was able to convey qualities not commonly attributed to utilitarian objects. "Any important art coming out of the industrial age," she wrote, "will draw inspiration from industry, because industry is alive and vital. The beauty of industry lies in its truth and simplicity. Every line is essential and therefore beautiful."

Among Bourke-White's most striking images is the one titled *Ammonia Gas Tanks*. In the picture she presented the enormous tanks as objects to be appreciated for their aesthetic qualities as well as for their function. That she took the picture while men, dwarfed by the structure, were toiling atop them, was not accidental. By doing so, Bourke-White deliberately illustrated another belief of those who championed industrial progress. That was the conviction that no matter how huge or complex an industrial object was, it could be controlled by human beings.

Bourke-White's fellow photographer Charles Sheeler was also motivated by the shapes of structures that he found all around him. Sheeler's most masterful pictures were those he took in the late 1920s under commission of the Ford Motor Company. Ford's main manufacturing facility, called River Rouge, was located just outside of Detroit. It was the largest industrial complex in the world. The photographs that Sheeler took there were of men working amidst enormous machinery, of elevated crosswalks that connected operating areas, and of towering smokestacks and gigantic blast furnaces.

Sheeler pursued a dual career as both an artist and a photographer. His paintings, which established him as one of America's most talented and respected artists, often focused on the beauty he saw in the lines and shadows contained in such simple objects as barns and staircases. This emphasis on shapes characterized his industrial photographs as well.

Like Margaret Bourke-White, Esther Bubley also produced masterful industrial photographs in which she conveyed man's control of even the most towering and complex machinery and equipment. Bubley's *Tomball Gasoline Plant* is a photograph that goes beyond an eye-arresting industrial image. It is a most human picture as well, taking the

viewer into a specific aspect of the human experience.

As such, Bubley's photograph is representative of the power of photographs in print, for among photography's greatest attributes is its ability to convey experiences we all share. Thanks to news photos, photo essays, and all other forms of photographs in print, this sharing of human experiences has become an almost daily occurrence.

Esther Bubley. *Tomball Gasoline Plant,* 1945.

Bubley first made her mark as an FSA photographer. She solidified her photographic career by producing dramatic industrial photographs such as this one in Tomball, Texas.

Chapter Seven
War Photography

Many of the most emotionally affecting photographs have been taken during armed conflict. In this picture, taken during the Korean War by U.S. Army Signal Corps photographer Al Chang, a man comforts a fellow soldier who has just witnessed the death of a close friend.

It is a sad fact of history that the story of almost every nation is filled with its participation in numerous and often tragic wars. Since the early 1850s, barely a dozen years after the birth of photography, the camera has been on the scene to record these conflicts. By the early days of the 20th century, in fact, photographers had become so numerous and so visible on the battlefield that during the 1912 Balkan War, King Ferdinand of Bulgaria complained, "This photography is not a profession. It is a disease."

The first war photographs were taken by a Rumanian, Carol Baptiste de Szathmary, who in 1853 captured images of conflict between Russia and Turkey over Wallachia and other Rumanian territory. His coverage was limited and the pictures were not widely distributed. The dispute that de Szathmary witnessed soon grew into a much larger conflict. Known as the Crimean War (1853–56), it pitted English, French, Turkish, and Sardinian troops against Russian forces in a fight over the control of the Black Sea province of Crimea. This war became the first to be recorded with a significant number of pictures. They were taken by an Englishman, Roger Fenton, who is recognized as the world's first major war photographer.

When the war erupted, Fenton, who had studied law and then had become a landscape photographer, saw an opportunity to record the conflict. His undertaking was officially approved by the British government and was funded by a commercial publisher, both of which had specific reasons for doing so. Opponents of the war at home in England had spread stories of the horrible condition of the British troops in the Crimea. Queen Victoria and the English government were hopeful that Fenton's pictures would disprove these stories. The publisher, Thomas Agnew, hoped that books and individual prints of Fenton's pictures would be profitable offerings. For political and commercial motives, it was understood that no pictures would be made of dead bodies, the wounded, soldiers dying of cholera, and other devastating situations that a few newspaper correspondents had been describing for a year or more.

In order to carry out the first major recording of an armed conflict, Fenton and two assistants journeyed to the Crimea by boat, taking with them five cameras, 700 glass plates, developing chemicals, tools, and rations of food. Fenton also took a specially constructed wagon that was fitted out as a

Roger Fenton used this wagon to transport his heavy equipment throughout the Crimea. He also used it as a darkroom to develop his wet plate negatives.

darkroom. He often found himself in real danger, particularly when shells exploded around the highly visible wagon. Fenton's photography was limited by the size and weight of his equipment, and by the collodion wet plate process that he used to make his glass-plate negatives. He had to prepare, expose (for no less than three seconds under the best of conditions, most often 10 seconds or more), and develop the plates on the spot. As a result, he could not take action pictures. Instead, his pictures showed soldiers, camps, trenches, and fortifications. They also revealed the aftermath of the fighting. Some of his photographs showed the ground littered with cannonballs that had killed 600 English cavalrymen in an area called The Valley of the Shadow of Death. It was this slaughter that was later made famous by Alfred, Lord Tennyson in his poem "The Charge of the Light Brigade.

Typical of the pictures that Fenton produced is his *Camp of the Fifth Dragoon Guards.* The picture reveals the experience Fenton had gained in producing large-scale landscape photographs before coming to the Crimea. It is an image that tells us as much about the Crimean terrain as about the military campaign.

After a year in the Crimea, Fenton was seriously sick with cholera and returned to England for treatment and recuperation, bringing with him 360 glass-plate negatives. His pictures were displayed both at the Royal Photographic Society and the Victoria and Albert Museum. But the public was sick and tired of the war and the special taxes imposed upon them to pay for

Roger Fenton.
Camp of the Fifth Dragoon Guards, 1855.

Fenton's photographs of the Crimean War were taken before it was possible to capture motion with a camera. However, the many compelling pictures he took of military camps before, between, and after battles have earned him recognition as the world's first major war photographer.

it, and the pictures did not sell. In 1862, Fenton suddenly, and apparently without explanation, gave up photography and began practicing law. Eventually a group of his negatives was purchased by Francis Frith, who published two small books with prints of the images pasted in.

Only five years after the Crimean War began, a much greater conflict captured the world's attention. The American Civil War was the most costly and tragic event in the history of the United States. Before the war ended, some 623,000 men were killed and hundreds of thousands of others were wounded.

More photographs were taken during the Civil War than had been taken in any previous armed conflict. Some 300 cameramen photographed the activities of the Northern army alone. Among the lesser-known but talented of these photographers were George Cook, Thomas C. Roche, Samuel A. Cooley, Jacob F. Coonley, and three brothers from Pennsylvania, A. J., S. L., and J. L. Bergstresser. The most important and productive photographers of the Civil War, however, were those hired and directed by Mathew B. Brady.

In 1861, when the Civil War began, Brady had already established himself as America's premier photographer through the hundreds of daguerreotypes, cartes-de-visite, cabinet photos, and other portraits his studios produced and displayed. As soon as the hostilities started he became determined to organize a team of photographers, equip them, and send them into the field to capture every aspect of the war. Only three days after receiving President Abraham Lincoln's permission to do so, Brady began to establish photographic bases in the various war zones and to assign members of his team to each of these areas.

Throughout the entire course of the war, from 1861 to 1865, Brady's camera corps produced tens of thousands of photographs. Like Fenton, they used the wet plate process and so could not take action pictures. However, they recorded almost everything else, often first with a full-plate camera and then again with a stereograph camera. The negatives were developed on the spot, and the photographers kept field records—notes on the date, location, situation or event, and the people in the pictures. Couriers collected the glass negatives and the field records at intervals and carried them to Brady's headquarters in Washington, D.C. There the pictures were catalogued, prints were made, and captions and descriptive text were written, based on the photographers' notes. *Harper's Weekly* had a

The Civil War introduced the world to the largest weapons that had ever been used. These weapons and the soldiers who manned them were favorite subjects for photographers who recorded the conflict.

Photographic portraits have always revealed more than simple likenesses. Portraits taken during the Civil War, such as this daguerreotype from about 1864, disclose the incredible youth of many of the soldiers on both sides of the conflict.

contract for the use of Brady pictures and published more than 1,000 of them as wood engravings accompanying news articles.

The Civil War photographers captured thousands of images of soldiers and their officers as they relaxed in camp or drilled during long lulls between battles. Many of their most dramatic pictures were of the extensive artillery batteries and of the men who operated some of the largest weapons the world had ever known. They also took scores of photographs of the sailors and the ships that were part of the naval aspect of the conflict. Field hospitals, long lines of supply wagons, acres of piled-up munitions, military trains, hastily erected bridges, telegraph corpsmen—everything that had to do with the war was photographed.

The pictures they took revealed the extraordinary youth of the men in both armies. They also disclosed the incredible human price paid by both sides. The most haunting of all their photographs were those of individual soldiers dead in the forest or behind sandbags and earth embankments, and of long rows of dead lying beside stone walls or in open fields immediately after battle. People had never seen such stark, devastating images before. The reality of the photograph made the horror of war inescapable.

That was true, too, of the images of Southern cities left in ruins by advancing Northern troops. Arguably the most powerful of these pictures was a photograph of the Confederate capital of Richmond, Virginia, taken in 1865 by Timothy O'Sullivan after Northern troops and artillery had devastated the city. The scope of the destruction, which was O'Sullivan's reason for taking the picture, is obvious. The photograph is made more compelling by the presence of the two women garbed in black. The all-black clothing was not unusual for the day, but their dress, particularly that of the hooded figure, can also be seen as a symbol of mourning for the destruction and the loss of a way of life. And one wonders if it was an accident that O'Sullivan's picture highlights the stirring of life among the ruins.

There has always been controversy over how many of the Civil War photographs Mathew Brady actually took himself. We know that many of the images were captured by Timothy O'Sullivan, George Gibson, John Reekie, David Knox, and George Barnard. We know also that thousands of others were taken by Alexander Gardner and his son James. The Gardners took so many outstanding photographs during the conflict that when the war was over they were able to publish 100 of them in two volumes titled *The Photographic Sketchbook of the Civil War.*

As for Brady, in 1861 he did take some photographs during the first Battle of Bull Run, in Virginia, near Washington. His greatest contribution, however, was in keeping most of his team together, motivating and directing them, and going deeply into debt to finance the operation. He also did the public a great service by exhibiting

Timothy O'Sullivan. Ruins in Richmond, Virginia, 1865.

By the end of the Civil War, many of the great cities of the American South had been destroyed. Viewers around the world were shocked by the photographic record of the devastation the war had caused.

many of the pictures in his Washington studio. Said one newspaper, "Mr. Brady has [brought] home to us the terrible reality and earnestness of war. Crowds of people are constantly going up the stairs [of the gallery]. Follow them and you will find them bending over photographic views of the fearful battlefield, taken immediately after the action."

Brady had hoped that once the war was over he would be able to sell enough of the photographs to the government to cover the heavy costs he had incurred in carrying out his operations. But the government, anxious to put the bitter war behind it, did not respond in the way he had hoped. In January 1896, mired in poverty, he died as a result of injuries suffered when he was struck by a horsedrawn streetcar. It was a sad end to what had been a brilliant career.

The limitations that the wet plate process imposed on Roger Fenton and the Civil War photographers were eliminated with the coming of dry plates and film in the 1870s and 1880s, and by the first decade

of the 1900s technical advances in photographic equipment had brought additional significant changes. There were now a number of small hand-held cameras available that made moving quickly from one scene of military action to another easier than ever before. Faster film emulsions and accurate shutters made it possible to photograph action of all kinds. In addition, the rise of photographic news magazines made demands for pictures of wartime action greater than ever before. All of these advancements and developments came into play in the years between 1914 and 1945 when nations from around the globe became immersed in two world wars.

In 1914, political disputes in Europe that could not be resolved ignited a war that pitted two giant alliances of nations against each other. On one side were the Central Powers (Germany, Austria-Hungary, Turkey, and Bulgaria). On the other side of the conflict were the Allied Powers (Great Britain, France, Italy, and Russia). In 1917, the United States was drawn into what

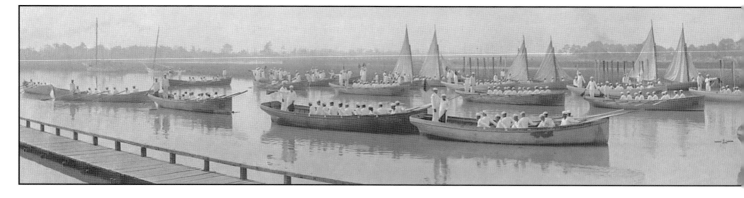

became known as World War I on the side of the Allied Powers.

World War I marked the first time that armies established their own official photographic units, usually as part of their existing signal corps, whose sole task was to document the conflict. The photographs that these cameramen were allowed to take, however, were tightly controlled. The governments of the warring nations, anxious to keep morale up at home, often forbade the photographers from taking pictures of the dead and dying and often prevented them from showing their troops suffering a defeat.

In 1939, the major nations of the world went to war again. Unlike World War I, which was fought entirely in Europe, World War II was a truly global conflict, with battle zones around the world. The war pitted Germany, Japan, and Italy, countries seeking world power, against England, France, Russia, and, beginning in 1941, the United States. Before the conflict was over, some 70 million soldiers, sailors, and air-

men were involved and more than 45 million people, including millions of civilians, were killed.

More pictures were taken during World War II than in any other conflict, exceeding by far those taken in the Civil War. In addition to the work of photographers in every military service, countless other pictures were taken by newspaper photographers from around the globe, and by men and women employed by the world's picture magazines and news and photo agencies.

A significant number of World War II photographers had previously experienced the horrors of armed conflict. The Hungarian-born Robert Capa, for example, had established himself as arguably the world's premier war photographer through the dramatic images he had captured during both the Spanish Civil War (1936–37) and the Japanese invasion of China (1938). In World War II, the photographs that Capa took in Europe, along with those taken by W. Eugene Smith in the Pacific, set a standard for all photographers who covered the conflict. Many of these cameramen—and women—had a special motivation for taking their World War II photographs. This motivation was expressed by Edward Steichen, who stated, "If we could really photograph war as it was, . . . in all its monstrous actuality, that could be a great deterrent to war." Steichen himself played an important role in the conflict. Rejected by the United States Army because it felt he was too old, Steichen was accepted by the Navy. Commissioned a lieutenant commander, he organized a photographic unit that captured dramatic images of the naval and aerial aspects of battles in the South Pacific.

Their ability to capture motion enabled World War I photographers to compile some of the most dramatic war images ever taken. In this photograph from 1918, the cameraman froze the action at the moment a soldier was about to be felled by poison gas.

Many of the pictures that Steichen's photographic unit took went beyond that of recording the war. They were outstanding photographs in and of themselves. Such a picture is that of crew members of an aircraft carrier awaiting the return of the planes and air men they had launched into battle (page 115). The photograph, taken by Wayne Miller, is marked by the photographer's use of the waning light of day to capture the men in silhouette. A portion of a propeller in the left foreground emphasizes the setting. A dramatic element is provided by the way Miller captured the crew members in postures clearly indicating their concern as they anxiously waited to learn the fate of their comrades.

As in World War I, the governments of the various warring nations tried to control the types of pictures the World War II photographers took or their editors published. No photographs of dead United States soldiers, for example, were released to the public until late in the conflict. Some pictures presented as "on the spot" action scenes actually were posed. Others were cropped by the photographer—or more usually by editors—to achieve the most dramatic effect. But the vast majority of World War II images were authentic, taken by combat photographers and accredited war correspondents who accompanied the troops into battle.

One of the major outcomes of World War II, as far as photography was concerned, was the way in which people throughout the world came to expect to see photographs taken in the heat of battle. Robert Capa expressed it this way: "If your pictures aren't good enough, you're not

close enough." The result was pictures that transported viewers directly into the action. The result also was the increased number of photographers who were killed while capturing their images. Capa himself died when he stepped on a land mine while covering the Indochina War in 1954.

Some of the most gripping photographs are those that depict the range of emotions displayed by both military participants and civilians affected by war. During World War II, for example, Toni Frissell captured an unforgettable image of a young boy sitting in front of his London home, which had just been destroyed by a German bomb (see page 113). His mother, father, and brother lay dead in the rubble. The expression that Frissell caught on the youngster's face speaks legions about the horrors of war and of the way in which even the most innocent civilians are affected by it.

Another photograph which, like the Frissell image, had enormous impact on the worldwide public when it was widely

G. L. Hall Optical Company. *Boat Exercises—Naval Training Station, Hampton Roads, Va.*, 1918.

Wartime photographers captured military preparations at home as well as battle abroad. This panoramic photograph shows one of the premier training centers for naval personnel during World War I.

During World War II, the intense interest on the part of the public to receive photographs of the action taking place around the world motivated manufacturers of cameras and film to produce even more advanced equipment. This ad from about 1943 was for a wartime Kodak camera.

Margaret Bourke-White: War Photographer

Through the pioneering industrial photographs she took for *Fortune* magazine and the photographs and photo essays she produced for *Life,* Margaret Bourke-White became one of the best-known magazine photographers of her time. She was one of the most prolific and accomplished war photographers as well.

Her combat assignments began in 1938 when *Life* sent her to Spain to photograph that nation's civil war. But it was during World War II when she took pictures of the action in Great Britain, North Africa, Italy, and Germany that she made her mark as a war photographer.

Bourke-White's World War II experience began in July 1941 when she went to Moscow on assignment from *Life* to photograph the German air raids that were wreaking havoc on that Russian city. She was the only non-Russian photographer to record the attacks. During one of the raids a bomb exploded near the roof of a building upon which she was photographing. She saved herself and her precious camera by diving through a skylight and falling shaken, but safe, to a floor below.

Two years later Bourke-White had an even more harrowing experience. She was aboard a troopship headed for the American and British invasion of North Africa when the ship was sunk by a torpedo from a German submarine. Although she spent a frightening night in a lifeboat in the middle of the ocean not knowing what daylight would bring, she managed to capture compelling photographs of her companions in the lifeboat.

Only a month after this experience she talked her way aboard the lead plane of a bomber group whose mission was to destroy the most important airfield in North Africa. She thus became the first woman ever to fly on a bombing run. Despite the fact that the temperature in the unheated plane, flying at 15,000 feet, was -40°F, she managed to keep her camera from freezing and took some of the most spectacular of all the bombing raid pictures produced during the war. *Life* printed them in a long story titled "*Life's* Bourke-White Goes Bombing."

During the rest of the conflict Bourke-White took thousands of pictures in various European theatres of operation, most notably in Italy's Cassino Valley, the site of some of the bitterest fighting of the war. Her most memorable pictures, however, were taken in the spring of 1945, shortly before the war in Europe ended. On April 11th she accompanied troops led by General George Patton as they entered the German concentration camp at Buchenwald where thousands of Jews and others had been slaughtered by the Nazis. Describing what she encountered as "more than the mind could grasp," she took pictures of naked corpses and starving camp survivors that, when published around the world, became forever embedded in the memory of all who saw them. Later she photographed other concentration camps, entering one even before American troops arrived.

After the war, Bourke-White was asked to describe what motivated her to take such horrifying pictures. "Difficult as these things may be to report or photograph," she replied, "it is something we war correspondents must do. We are in a privileged and sometimes unhappy position. We see a great deal of the world. Our obligation is to pass it on to others."

printed in newspapers and magazines was a picture taken by U. S. Army Signal Corps photographer Al Chang during the Korean War (1950–53), fought by North Korea, supported by China, against South Korea, aided by United States and other United Nations troops. The photograph (page 104) captures the scene as an American soldier is comforted by a fellow Marine moments after learning that his best friend has been killed. The inclusion in the picture of the third Marine paying close attention to his book in order to give his comrades their moment of privacy adds to the poignancy of the photograph.

As far as photographers were concerned, the deadliest conflict in history was the Vietnam War, fought in the 1960s and the first half of the 1970s between communist North Vietnam and United States—backed South Vietnam. During this long and divisive war, more than 70 North Vietnamese photographers were killed, and more than 135 cameramen and camerawomen from other nations lost their lives.

Among photographers from around the globe who recorded the conflict were two South Vietnamese brothers, Huynh Thanh My and Huynh Cong Ut, both of whom took pictures for the Associated Press. In 1972 Huynh Cong ("Nick") Ut captured a photograph of children running away from an American-aided napalm bomb attack in South Vietnam. Eventually awarded the Pulitzer Prize, the highest honor a photograph can receive, the picture is regarded by many as the single most powerful image taken during the entire war. It is also viewed as one of the most influential war photographs ever taken. Its impact was most eloquently described by the American writer Sally Quinn: "When people who had been for the war saw the picture, they thought 'Oh my God, what are we doing?' It was the beginning of the end of the war. For all the words that had been written about Vietnam, there was nothing that had the power of this picture."

By the time the Vietnam War was fought, television had come to play an important role in the lives of millions. Increasingly it became the major way that countless people obtained their news. Television, however, has not diminished the importance of the war photograph. Television reportage, no matter how immediate and dramatic, appears on the screen for a few moments and then is gone. A war photograph, like all still pictures, has a permanence that allows it to be studied and considered over and over again. This vital attribute of the war photograph was clearly evident in the coverage of more recent conflicts such as the Persian Gulf War, the hostilities in Bosnia and Kosovo, and in other armed confrontations around the world. What has become clear is that there is no more powerful or lasting means of visually recording the heroism, the indomitable human spirit, and the triumph and tragedy of armed conflict than the war

Toni Frissell. Boy in ruins of his house, 1945.

"The story of my life," wrote Frissell, "is told in terms of photographs I have taken, places I have visited, and people I have met. This is as it should be. A photographer keeps a biographical record with every new assignment and the photographer's subjects help shape her destiny."

Huynh Cong ("Nick") Ut. Children running from bombing attack, 1972.

This photograph of children running in terror from a napalm bombing attack has become a symbol of the horror and frustration of the Vietnam War. It is yet another reminder of the power that photography has in influencing peoples' thoughts and opinions.

photograph: ·

World War II in Pictures

The extraordinary number of photographs taken during World War II revealed all aspects of the first truly global conflict in history. Robert Capa gained international fame for combat pictures such as the one shown here of a soldier pinned down by enemy fire during the Allied invasion of German-held France. A German photographer captured Nazi troops parading before German dictator Adolph Hitler shortly before Germany launched all-out attacks on its neighboring countries. The images of the fighter plane returning to its carrier base and the carrier crewmen on deck are two of the tens of thousands of pictures taken by members of Edward Steichen's Naval Aviation Photographic Unit. Joe Rosenthal's picture of the American flag being raised at Iwo Jima has become the most famous of all World War II images.

Robert Capa. Normandy invasion, 1944.

Photographer unknown.
Nazi troops, 1942.

Photographer unknown.
American soldier administering blood plasma, 1945.

Charles Kerlee.
Fighter plane returning to carrier, 1945.

Barrett Gallagher.
Carrier crewmen on deck, 1943.

Joe Rosenthal.
Iwo Jima flag raising, 1945.

Chapter Eight

Photographs in Color

Hand-coloring a daguerreotype was a delicate process. But many skilled daguerreotype artists were able to produce images of great beauty, including this one from about 1850.

This color photograph of activity in a street on New York City's East Side was taken by photographer Henry Peabody of the Detroit Publishing Company. The color image was produced through an early color electro-printing process that the company used some 30 years before the development of color film made color photography practical for almost everyone.

From the time that scientists and inventors began their attempts to produce a permanent photographic image, one of their main goals was to capture pictures in color. In describing his earliest experimentations to his brother, for example, Nicephore Niépce, who in 1826 succeeded in producing the first photographic image, stated emphatically, "I must succeed in fixing the colors." Louis Daguerre felt that, despite his enormous triumph in producing the first usable photographic process, it was not a complete success, because daguerreotypes were unable to capture images in natural color.

Daguerreotypists who took their cameras outdoors knew that there would be a large market for scenes in color. By the mid 1840s, the public, which only five years earlier had been thrilled simply to be recorded in a photograph, was increasingly expressing a yearning for likenesses in color. In response, photographers tried to use paints, crayons, and colored pencils to hand-color the images their cameras produced. What they soon learned was that hand-painting daguerreotypes was a tedious and very difficult undertaking. Few had the artistic skill

for the task. In addition, the daguerreotype image was very delicate and easily damaged by a careless brushstroke. They solved their problem by turning to a whole new type of craftsman—the hand-coloring expert.

In the United States, where the daguerreotype gained its greatest popularity, hand-coloring by specialists became a common practice. Several books on the subject were published, providing instruction on how to get the best results from watercolors, pastels, and colored crayons. During the daguerreotype era, the American Artists' Association, an organization made up exclusively of professional colorists, was formed.

As the daguerreotype was replaced by new forms of photographs, many colorists turned to hand-painting ambrotypes and tintypes. During the American Civil War, when many soldiers carried tintypes of their loved ones, a colored tintype was an especially treasured possession.

The first person to make a photographic presentation of the principles on which all color photography would eventually be based was the British physicist James Clerk Maxwell, who built on the early 19th-century work of Thomas Young and Hermann

was a black-and-white positive image contact printed from a negative that had been photographed with a container of either red, green, or blue liquid in front of the lens, which acted as filters. In front of each projector Maxwell placed the same liquid filter used to take each picture. When the red, green, and blue projected images were adjusted to overlap in register, the picture on the screen was imperfect, but unmistakably in color.

Maxwell's achievement provided inspiration to scores of individuals who were attempting to capture an effective color image. In the last decades of the 1800s, several innovators—most notably Louis Ducos du Hauron and Charles Cos in France and John Joly in Ireland—conducted many experiments using various types of color screens and filters. The importance of their work lies in their attempts to make glass plates selectively color sensitive for exposure in the camera. This would be a long step up from Maxwell's cumbersome liquid filters.

In 1904 an important advance took place with the introduction of a black-and-white emulsion that was sensitive to all colors (called *panchromatic* sensitivity). This emulsion made it possible, later that same year, for two French brothers, Louis and Auguste Lumière, to achieve the long-sought-after goal of capturing color on a single plate in a camera. They accomplished this by using small grains of potato starch that were transparent enough to serve as tiny color filters. A mixture of equal amounts of grains dyed orange, green, or violet (essentially equivalent to primary red, green, and blue) was coated onto a glass plate along with the new emulsion. When exposed and processed, the result was

Before the collodion process became popular for making wet plate negatives, it was used for making positives on glass. The glass plates could be inserted into a special lantern slide projector and shown on a wall, screen, or other flat surface. Many viewers were introduced to the marvels of color photography by viewing lantern slides such as this one from about 1910.

von Helmholtz. In 1861 Maxwell delivered a dramatic demonstration that any color could be recreated by mixing red, blue, and green light in varying proportions. Before a gathering at the Royal Institution of London, Maxwell projected three lantern slides of a plaid ribbon upon a screen. He used a separate projector for each slide. Each slide

a full-color slide. Plates were made in standard sizes, 3 1/4 by 4 1/4 inches and larger.

The Lumières patented their plates under the name *Autochrome* in 1904 and three years later began manufacturing them for sale. Photographers around the world rushed to adopt the new process. In that same year, Alfred Stieglitz introduced this new miracle of photography to America through a major exhibition of autochromes taken by himself, Edward Steichen, and another Photo-Secessionist, Frank Eugene. For the next three decades the Lumières' process, although somewhat limited in choice of subject by the long exposure time required, dominated color photography.

In the mid 1930s a breakthrough took place that would do for color photography what George Eastman's Kodak camera had done for photography itself. Just as the Kodak placed the camera in the hands of millions, the introduction of *Kodachrome* film made taking pictures in color possible for almost everyone.

The invention of Kodachrome film was due, in great measure, to the efforts of two young men, Leopold Mannes and Leopold Godowsky. Both men were talented musicians. Mannes was a third-generation member of the Damrosch family, which made major contributions to the development of serious music in the United States, and whose parents established the world-famous Mannes School of Music in New York City. He would become a celebrated concert pianist, would write acclaimed chamber and orchestral music, and would inspire countless future musicians through his teaching. Godowsky was an accomplished violinist who, among other musical achievements, would hold chairs in both

Heinrich Kühn. *Group*, 1908.

The autochrome, one of the first forms of color photography, allowed photographers to produce delicate, beautiful images. The German photographer Heinrich Kühn was an early master of the autochrome.

the San Francisco Symphony Orchestra and the Los Angeles Philharmonic.

The two Leopolds met at Riverdale Country School in New York. They quickly discovered that they shared not only a passion for music but for invention as well. After attending a physics class in which the instructor explained the challenges faced in achieving an easy-to-use form of color photography, they joined forces to attack the problem.

The school gave them permission to use its physics laboratory and Mannes's parents

allowed them to work weekends in an unused kitchen in the family's apartment. Their early experiments, which centered around inventing a camera that could effectively capture color images, were interrupted when Mannes went off to Harvard and Godowsky enrolled at the University of California. In 1922, after each had graduated, Godowsky returned to the East Coast and they resumed their experiments in earnest. By this time they had decided upon a whole new approach. They came to the conclusion that the answer to attaining a practical means of color photography was to be found not with a different kind of camera, but with a whole new kind of film. Their specific goal became that of perfecting a film coated with three layers of emulsion each sensitive to one of the primary colors of light: red, green, and blue.

By 1930 Mannes and Godowsky had gone a long way toward achieving this goal. There were still many refinements to be made, but the young partners were out of money and needed more sophisticated equipment. These obstacles were removed when officials at the Kodak Research Laboratory invited them to work with the Kodak staff and to take advantage of the laboratory's facilities.

By 1935 Mannes, Godowsky, and their colleagues at Kodak had perfected a film that produced full-color positive images when it was processed. Called Kodachrome, it was released for use in 16mm movie cameras and soon thereafter in 35mm size for use in still cameras. In order to process this new film it was necessary to use three different color developers. However, in 1936 Germany's Agfa Company introduced a film called Agfachrome that required only a single color developer.

More improvements in color quickly followed. Between 1939 and 1943, both the Agfa Company and Eastman Kodak introduced new color negative films, from which prints were made, and advanced printing paper that greatly improved the quality of color prints. Yet even with these advancements, all color processing printing had to be carried out by a commercial photofinisher.

Then, in the years 1947–50, Eastman Kodak introduced three new products that made color photography processing and printing available to everyone. One of these products was a color negative film called Ektacolor. The second was a matching, easy-to-use printing paper. The third was a more convenient, high-quality slide film called Ektachrome. All could be processed by the photographer.

Although most professional photographers still preferred to have processing and

printing done by a commercial firm, these products and others introduced shortly thereafter by several companies, including Fuji of Japan, created an enormous increase in amateur color photography. As a result of this continued flow of products and processes, the vast majority of pictures were soon being taken in color.

Perhaps the greatest challenge that color presents to the photographer is the beauty of color itself. The temptation is great to capture a blaze of hues in the belief that color alone will make an outstanding picture. But just as tonal range alone does not make a great black-and-white picture, it is not colors themselves but the photographer's sensitive use of them that produces a fine photograph. Some of the most masterful of all color images are those composed of subtle tones with carefully selected accents of color. As photographer Edward Weston, a master of both black-and-white

and color photography once stated, "Those who say that color photography, will eventually replace black and white are talking nonsense. They are different means to different ends."

Despite the challenges of color photography, many photographers have become masters of the approach. They have, for example, been able to produce color images that feature striking textures, designs, and patterns. Certain of those photographers have effectively used specific colors in their images to express emotions and feelings evoked by the subject in front of their camera. Others have been able to use color to convey the feeling of light and atmosphere in special and exciting ways.

One of the greatest of the early modern masters of the color image was Eliot Porter, a man whose photographic contributions were made after an abrupt change in

Photographer unknown. Boating party, 1915.

A number of Japanese photographers were among those who, in the early 20th century, worked toward achieving an efficient means of color photography. Their work was marked by the way they used color to enhance the graceful presentation of their subjects.

Eliot Porter. *Great Spruce Head Island, Maine,* about 1955.

Porter had a lifelong interest in birds. His color photographs of them, taken with long-distance lenses, are marked by their clarity and the way he was able to "arrest" his subjects in flight.

Jan Groover. *Still Life,* 1968.

Groover has become known for complex and innovative color still lifes. The beauty of her images is enhanced by her use of the platinum print process.

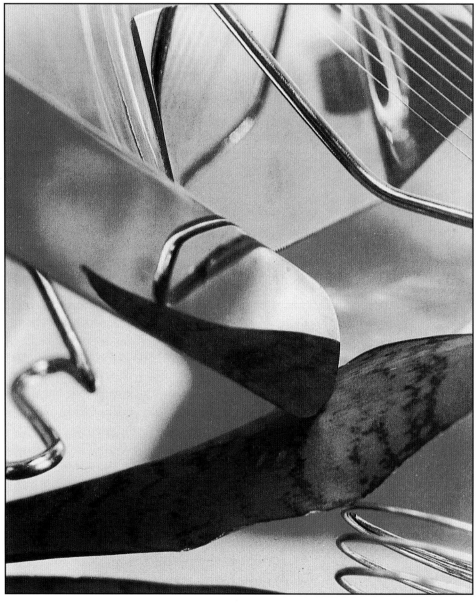

careers. After graduating from Harvard Medical School in 1924, Porter taught biochemistry and bacteriology at the school for several years. During his student days he had begun taking photographs and in 1939 Alfred Stieglitz presented an exhibition of Porter's work. The acclaim that these images received changed Porter's life. He gave up science and medicine and devoted himself to photography.

Porter was an avowed naturalist. His images are distinguished by the way in which he was able to capture various shadings of light to accentuate the range of colors he found in natural objects like rocks and trees. Porter was also a master at tracing the delicate patterns and colors to be found in leaves and grasses. Above all, his work is marked by the discipline he brought to each of his images. He never photographed color simply for color's sake. Subtlety was his trademark, resulting in photographs that time and time again featured brilliant accents played against softer tones.

In more recent times, photographers such as William Eggleston, Jan Groover, and Joel Meyerowitz have become celebrated for the special ways in which they have used color. Eggleston is generally credited with having played a major role in the acceptance of color by some of its harshest detractors. As late as 1976 color had been ignored by many serious photographers and critics who regarded its use as trivializing the medium. But in that year New York's prestigious Museum of Modern Art went a long way toward "legitimizing" the use of color by mounting a solo exhibition of 75 of Eggleston's color prints. Critics hailed the way Eggleston, through the use of color, had captured images that were both lyrical and at the same time often mysterious.

The work of Jan Groover has been marked by the way in which she has carried on the approach of the artistic photographers who in the 1920s, '30s, and '40s brought a new, modernistic vision to photography. In the 1970s Groover made images primarily concerned with form and design, rather than literal content. Among other innovations, she often created pictures that present architectural details in three groups. For example, in one photograph the lower corner of a bronze door and the columns and steps that surrounded it are shown from three different distances and angles of view.

In the 1980s, Groover's concern with sculptural form led her to create a series of photographs in which manufactured goods are contrasted with natural objects. For example, household implements such as eggbeaters, spatulas, pie pans, and cups and saucers are presented alongside the leaves and blossoms of plants. In other photographs, common household utensils are arranged to reveal their form and structure by the play of ambient color reflected from their surfaces. Groover's work has continued to evolve and she is today regarded as one of the outstanding artists of color photography.

Like the photographs of Eliot Porter, Joel Meyerowitz's images are characterized by their contrasts and subtlety of tones. While Porter concentrated almost entirely on objects he found in nature, Meyerowitz has focused on a variety of subjects. He spent several years photographing the wide range of colors presented by urban street

life. He produced a compelling book made up entirely of pictures of red-headed people. But he has responded to nature, too. Another book focused on the beauty of wildflowers. Some of his most memorable work has used color to capture the beauty of light in the natural world.

The variations in illumination presented by sunlit beaches, dramatic sunrises and sunsets, and often spectacular storms on Cape Cod, Massachusetts, has provided Meyerowitz with scenes that are particularly appropriate for his mastery of light and shadow. Especially compelling is Meyerowitz's photograph *Bay/Sky, Provincetown* contained in *Cape Light,* one of many books that have featured his images. In the picture, Meyerowitz captured the soft pink hues of the clouds amid the remaining blue of the sky. The play of light on the water, on the lone person in the image, and on

(Continued on page 126)

Joel Meyerowitz. *Bay/Sky, Provincetown,* 1977.

Meyerowitz has said that the special sense of mood and light in his Cape Cod pictures was inspired by the paintings of some of his favorite artists, including Edward Hopper.

The Glory of Color

Since the time it became widely available, color photography has been applied to a great range of purposes. Initially it was used mainly for advertising and fashion photography; Louise Dahl-Wolfe was among the first fashion photographers to use color. Toward the end of the Farm Security Administration project (see page 86), documentary photographers such as Marion Post Wolcott began to capture their images in color. Although color was not much respected by the art world until the 1970s, contemporary photographers such as Ernst Haas, Andreas Gursky, and Joel Sternfeld have received critical acclaim for their innovative use of it. William Wegman, another prominent photographer (see page 141), uses color to emphasize the details in his humorous photographs.

Marion Post Wolcott.
Children fishing, Anniston, Alabama, 1940.

Louise Dahl-Wolfe.
The Covert Look, 1949.

Ernst Haas.
New York skyline, 1975.

William Wegman.
Harvest, 1994.

Joel Sternfeld.
McLean, VA, December 1978.

Andreas Gursky.
Chicago Board of Trade, 1997.

Bob Krist. *Mount Orgueil Castle,*
about 1995.

*This photograph of a castle in
England's Channel Islands is one of
thousands of images that have made
Krist one of the most successful of all of
today's travel photographers. "I am particularly fond of photographing at dusk
or twilight, when the sky is still a rich
blue before it turns black," states Krist.*

the sailing vessel in the far background add
to the impact of the image. The most dramatic feature is the effect created by the
stark white and red of the small boat in the
foreground contrasted with the darkening
sand upon which it lies.

Many of today's most accomplished
color photographers are men and women
who make their living by carrying out
assignments for picture magazines. One of
the most talented and successful of these is
Bob Krist, who photographs for *National
Geographic, Travel & Leisure, Gourmet,* and

other publications. His work has produced
stunning images made on assignments that
have taken him around the world from the
United States to Malaysia.

Keenly aware of the special demands
and challenges faced by those who make
their living by hopping from one often
hastily decided upon assignment to another, Krist also spends considerable time
teaching. He offers his students the following advice: "Once you leave your quiet,
organized, and orderly studio, you find that
chaos reigns supreme. It is a jungle out
there, full of wondrous discoveries, as well
as pitfalls and unforeseen obstacles. A lot of
what happens to you depends on both how
versatile and well prepared you are to deal
with the unknown and how quickly you
can react and improvise."

Typical of the way in which Krist is able
to adapt to all conditions and sometimes
surprise himself with the way both natural
and artificial light can transform a scene is
his experience in producing the striking
image of Orgueil Castle on England's
Channel Islands. Describing his shooting of
the picture, he writes, "What is great about
dusk is that no matter how bad the weather
is, the sky will eventually turn blue for a
while after sunset. . . . I'd been battling gray,
rainy skies all day on Jersey and I was
scheduled to move on to another island the
next day. Despite the drizzle, I set up my
tripod across the harbor from the castle and
waited for dusk. I knew that the town's
neon signs and streetlights would glow
nicely, but I was pleasantly surprised by
how wonderful the castle, illuminated with
floodlights, looked."

Jay Maisel. Boy blowing bubble, about 1985.

Maisel's photographs appear in magazines and advertisements as well as in art galleries. Widely traveled, he photographs only in color. "I see in color," he says. "Everyone does."

Like Bob Krist, Jay Maisel is one of the busiest of today's photographers. Working exclusively in color, Maisel's images are marked by an elegant simplicity of both color and form and by the painterly qualities he brings to them.

Although he photographs around the world, Maisel's great passion is capturing powerful and beautiful photographs of the United States. Speaking of this endeavor, which he has pursued for three decades, he states, "An all-inclusive view of America would be a never-ending task. By the time you finish one end the other needs work. Patterns emerge in terms of form and content. Light changes and may be better down the road, or later on, or in another season or another place. So the task continues."

Maisel has a special ability to capture people in interesting poses. His picture of a boy blowing a bubble is such an image, made even more compelling by the dramatic contrast of the young man's bright yellow clothing with the red and green wall.

Aside from the influence color photography has had on the work of photographers, its impact in many other areas has been profound. Color photography, for example, changed the whole world of advertising. Through color images, manufacturers are able to appeal to potential customers in more enticing ways than once thought possible. Color photography has also had a dramatic impact on the world of art. Before the advent of color, students were forced to study the works of the great masters in black and white. Now color slides, transparencies, and prints make it possible to examine great paintings in all

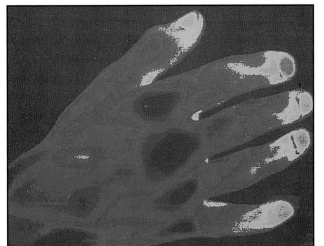

Photography has enabled the medical profession to make far more advanced diagnoses than once thought possible. This thermogram from about 1995 reveals that the fingers on this patient's hand are warmest while the knuckles are coolest.

their glory no matter where the original paintings are housed. Today, the public has become so accustomed to seeing pictures in color that most newspapers print their feature news and sports photographs in color.

Some of the most spectacular uses of color have been made possible by continued advances in modern technology. Sophisticated computers, for example, are now used to enhance photographs in such

Photography has profoundly changed our vision of the universe. Astronauts, armed with cameras, have given us spectacular pictures of man's travels beyond the earth's atmosphere such as this one of a space walk.

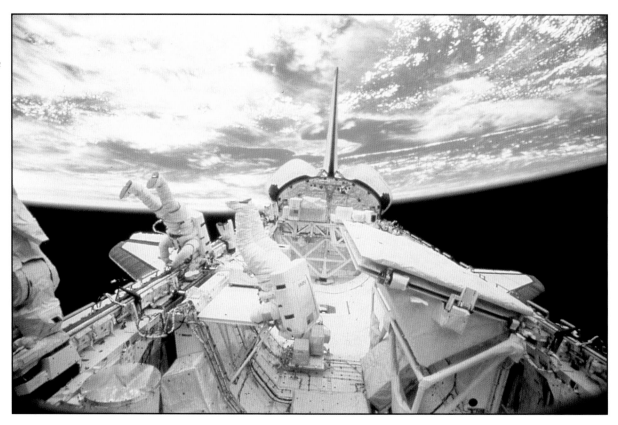

a way that features hidden or unclear to the naked eye are revealed. Patterns formed by specific colors in these photographs enable archaeologists to discover buried sites, military personnel to locate camouflaged areas, and geographers to produce the most accurate maps ever created. The world of medicine has also benefited greatly from the use of color photography. Computer-enhanced X rays, which permit different densities of bone, marrow, and tissue to be revealed through specific colors, have made medical diagnosis a more exact science than ever before. Scientists in some fields are now aided by what is called electrophotography. Using this process an object is placed on a sheet of unexposed film. A burst of electricity from a metal plate beneath the film

produces a picture that reveals, through various colors, properties of the object that otherwise might remain unknown.

Perhaps the most dramatic use of color has been its use in photographically probing the deep reaches of outer space. The extraordinary revelations made through color images taken by cameras in the hands of astronauts, or mounted on powered telescopes, or aboard space satellites has resulted in nothing less than a much deeper understanding of our universe. One can only imagine what the reaction of innovators like James Clark Maxwell, the Lumière brothers, or Leopold Mannes and Leopold Godowsky would be if they could see what their pioneering efforts in color photography have spawned.

Color Films and Papers

Color photography is based on the Young-Helmholtz three-color theory of vision. According to this theory, the central portion of the retina of the eye contains receptor cells called cones that are individually sensitive to one of the primary colors of light: red, green, or blue. When the cones are stimulated by various strengths of red, green, and blue wavelengths they send composite signals to the brain, which interprets them as all the colors we see.

Based on this theory, modern color film has three light-sensitive layers. One layer, containing blue-sensitive emulsion, is sensitive to blue light. Another layer, containing green-sensitive emulsion, is sensitive to green and blue light. A third layer, containing red-sensitive emulsion is sensitive to red and blue light.

Because all the emulsion layers are sensitive to blue, color films have a thin yellow filter layer under the top blue-sensitive layer to prevent blue wavelengths from reaching the green- and red-sensitive layers below (a yellow filter absorbs blue). When color film is exposed to light from a scene in front of the camera, each layer of film records only its own color. The film is then exposed to white light and developed so that dyes are produced in each emulsion layer. Any remaining silver in the emulsions is bleached out along with the yellow filter, leaving a full-color image. The processing of color print paper is essentially the same as that of the color film.

Modern Color Film

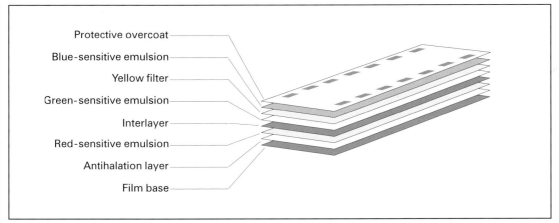

- Protective overcoat
- Blue-sensitive emulsion
- Yellow filter
- Green-sensitive emulsion
- Interlayer
- Red-sensitive emulsion
- Antihalation layer
- Film base

Color Photographic Paper

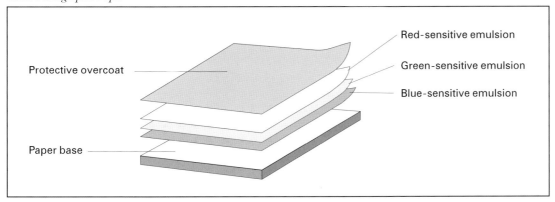

- Protective overcoat
- Paper base
- Red-sensitive emulsion
- Green-sensitive emulsion
- Blue-sensitive emulsion

Chapter Nine
Modern Photography

Sebastião Salgado. *Serra Pelada, Brazil's Klondike*, 1986.

Salgado captured dramatic images of men and women who, despite technological advancements, continue to work at hard labor. The photographs in his Workers *series, such as this one of a gold mine in Brazil, have been acclaimed as a visual tribute to labor and the human condition.*

In the 1960s, toward the end of his long photographic career, 84-year-old Edward Steichen expressed his opinion as to what lay ahead for the medium to which he had contributed so much. "In the past few years," he wrote, "there has been such a larger number of free-spirited, independently thinking young photographers—seekers, probers, and explorers of new horizons—than we have heretofore encountered. They give ample assurance that the future of photography is richer in prospect and potential than ever before."

Steichen has been proved correct. What he could have added, however, was the fact that photography's ability to remain an ever-changing, ever-growing medium is due not only to the skills and imaginations of modern-day photographers but also to the ways in which they have learned so much from those who have gone before them.

Paul Strand was one of those photographic giants whose work has both inspired and instructed scores of today's photographers. He captured thousands of images of people, places, and nature throughout the world. He was a most sensitive photographer who constantly sought to impart as much meaning to his images as possible. Speaking of his approach to taking pictures, for example, he stated, "It is one thing to photograph people; it is another to make others care about them by revealing the core of their humanness."

Strand's desire to give meaning to his images is often marked by the simplicity and directness of his pictures. Typical of most of his photographs is the picture titled *The Family, Luzzara, Italy, 1953*. Like so many of his images, it is a photograph characterized by such directness in both form and subject that it does not cause an immediate sensation. But as one studies it more closely, the sensitivity and the power of the picture become apparent.

The photograph is a masterpiece of composition, framed on one side by the man leaning against the building and on the other by the family member leaning against his bicycle. The group of three figures in the doorway presents a powerful focal point. The varying shapes and forms of the housefront and doorway, and the soft play of light contrasted with the dark interior beyond the entrance, add to the picture's appeal. So too does the way in which Strand was able

Paul Strand. *The Family, Luzzara, Italy, 1953.*

Through honest yet sensitive images, Strand offered proof of photography's ability to penetrate the human soul. "I have come," he wrote, "to value photography more and more for those things which it alone can accomplish."

to capture the differing expressions on the faces of the family members. That so many photographers working today have taken up the search for the elegant apparent simplicity that Strand achieved is the greatest testimony to the influence he exerted.

The work of Edward Weston has also had a profound impact on modern photography. A native of Illinois, Weston moved to California in 1911, where he opened his own photographic studio. Influenced by the pictorialists, his earliest photographs were artistic and sometimes abstract in nature. In the early 1920s, he went to Mexico along with fellow photographer Tina Modotti. There he changed his photographic approach. Abandoning pictorialism, he decided that what he really wanted to do was to photograph the world around him. "The camera," he wrote, "should be for a recording of life . . . whether it be polished steel or palpitating flesh."

In 1927, Weston returned permanently to California. He had a small portrait studio but devoted as much time as possible to personal work. He began to photograph

the extraordinary forms that he encountered along the Pacific coastline. Along with capturing magnificent landscape images, he also focused on specific natural objects. Almost everything in nature became a subject for his camera—tangled trees and stumps, rock formations, and shells. He saw beauty in every natural form, even in commonplace vegetables. To him, the delicate, precise overlapping of layers in an artichoke sliced down through the middle was as photographically intriguing as the towering mountains or crashing surf that were also objects of his camera.

Among Weston's most intriguing images is the picture titled *Burning Cypress Roots.* It is a photograph that exemplifies his ability to see things that others could not initially perceive. When Weston encountered the root, the pattern of the lines of growth made it appear as if it were on fire. He captured this feeling by photographing the root close-up from the angle that best conveyed his perception. As we study the image we can understand what renowned photographer Cecil Beaton meant when he stated that Edward Weston "succeeded with his passion, in making us see the world around us in his way."

Minor White was a photographer who believed that simple objects could be the basis for pictures that expressed the photographer's deepest feelings. He took an approach now embraced by many photographers. White's images contained a genuine sense of mystery. They were photographs that left it to the viewer to develop an understanding of what each image really meant. White's goals, he wrote, were "to photograph some things for what they are, and others for what else they are."

In further explaining this approach, White described it as a theory of *equivalents*, a term first used by Alfred Stieglitz. To White, "equivalents" meant dividing the experience a person has in viewing a photograph into three parts. The first part of the experience is the photograph itself. The second part is what takes place in the viewer's mind while observing the picture. The third part is the innermost feelings that come to the viewer when he or she later remembers the image.

The photograph White titled *Windowsill Daydreaming* is representative of his work. At first viewing it appears to be an image simply capturing various shapes and patterns formed on a wall by light pouring through an open window. But as far as White was concerned it was much more than that. In describing the image, he stated that while it captured a sight frequently seen, his purpose in taking the picture was to give viewers an opportunity to study it and to consider whether the image moved

Edward Weston. *Burning Cypress Roots*, 1945.

To Weston, these roots of a cypress tree seemed to be on fire. "All these forms are my neighbors," stated Weston. "If with clear vision I have seen more than the average person sees—well, that's my job."

them to recall more profound experiences in their lives. White was well aware that what he wished to accomplish through the photograph would be experienced by relatively few who saw it. But that, he felt, was sufficient. To him, any photograph that made viewers think and feel beyond the subject of the picture itself was well worth taking.

Many of the photographers who came to prominence in the last half of the 20th century owed their approach to the work of not one but of several photographers who came before them. Trained as an engineer, Harry Callahan became committed to photography after attending a workshop conducted by Ansel Adams and then studying with Laszlo Moholy-Nagy at the New Bauhaus in Chicago. His path toward eventually becoming known as "the photographer of the commonplace" was inspired in great measure by his appreciation of the work of Paul Strand. His decision to make the expression of his own inner feelings the basis for much of his photography came as the result of a lecture he attended given by Minor White.

Before his long career was over, Callahan became known for the scores of intriguing images of city life that he captured. He also produced striking nature studies. He broke new ground through the

Minor White. *Windowsill Daydreaming,* 1958.

White once defined his photographs as mirages, meaning that they were not what they appeared to be. His images challenge each viewer to bring his or her own interpretation to the picture.

imaginative use of multiple exposures to combine several views into a single picture. And he became a master of modern color photography.

Callahan's photograph of a weed reveals his fascination with line and form. It is a striking example of the way in which he was able to produce an intriguing image even when training his camera on the simplest of objects.

Like Harry Callahan's, the work of Aaron Siskind has had significant influence on scores of modern photographers. Siskind's career was marked by the complete about-face he took in his approach to the medium. Early on he concentrated on capturing starkly realistic images of such subjects as life in New York City's Harlem

and Bowery neighborhoods. But in the 1940s he began to take very different kinds of pictures.

Stating that "for the first time in my life subject matter as such . . . ceased to be of primary importance," Siskind began to concentrate on making abstract images. For the next two decades he took close-up photographs of everyday objects that are usually ignored. Focusing on the patterns he saw all around him, he photographed the designs on walls and discarded pieces of metal. He also captured intriguing designs created by oil and water stains on various textures of paper.

Siskind's approach went beyond influencing the work of many photographers who followed him. It also inspired designers in other fields who incorporated the shapes and patterns he captured into their own creations.

While Callahan and Siskind became heralded for the artistic qualities they brought with them, another mid-20th-century photographer, Robert Frank, gained acclaim for a very different type of photograph. Frank began his career as a fashion photographer and then entered the field of photojournalism, carrying out assignments for such magazines as *Life, Look,* and *Fortune.* Frank, however, who was endowed with a passionate sense of individuality, came to dislike working for others, particularly corporate-minded magazine publishers.

In 1955, with the aid of his friend Walker Evans, he applied for and received a Simon Guggenheim Memorial Fellowship, which enabled him to undertake a two-year photographic tour of the United

States. Using a 35mm camera he criss-crossed the nation capturing images of roadside bars, parades, automobiles, highways, gas stations, and billboards. Many of his pictures included the presence of the American flag hanging on buildings, adorning parade reviewing stands, and waving above large outings.

In many ways Frank's photographic journey was similar to that undertaken earlier by Evans for the Farm Security Administration. Both men were sensitive to how much the artifacts with which people surrounded themselves revealed about their way of life. But whereas Evans celebrated various aspects of American life, Frank's images were a far less positive portrayal.

In 1958 Frank's photographs were published in Paris in a book titled *Les Americains* and the next year as *The Americans* in the United States. Regarded by most reviewers as downbeat, the book at first elicited a negative reaction from much of the public as well. What those who railed against it failed to recognize was that in Frank's portrayal of loneliness and desperation there was also beauty and tenderness. Frank's own evaluation of what he had discovered and photographed was contained in his explanation of why he had taken his pictures in black and white instead of color. "Black and white," he stated, "is the vision of hope and despair."

In the next decade a dramatic turnaround took place. *The Americans* became nothing less than a bible to many of the thousands of those caught up in the youthful rebellion against the corporate culture, social inequity, and certain long-held values that was a major part of the 1960s. In the

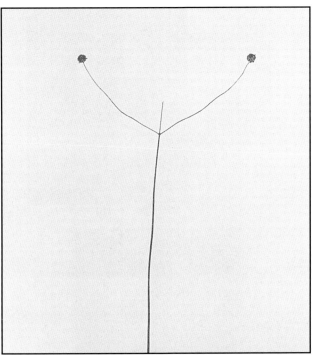

Harry Callahan. *Detroit,* about 1947.

In the hands of a masterful photographer, even the simplest object can be made to represent something beyond its natural form. In this Callahan photograph, a weed takes on an appearance both human and abstract.

Aaron Siskind. *Jerome, Arizona,* 1949.

When they first appeared, Siskind's images disturbed many photographers who felt they were more like abstract paintings than photographs. It was not long, however, before they came to be appreciated for what Siskind intended them to be—works of art and design that remain within the realm of photography.

Diane Arbus. King and queen of the ball, about 1967.

Arbus's images of subjects not commonly photographed include pictures of older people trying to appear younger than they are. This is her photograph of a couple who had been crowned king and queen of a senior citizens' ball.

Robert Frank. Political rally, 1956.

Frank believed that a photograph should be able to stand on its own without any text. Many of his photographs, such as this one of a tuba player at a political rally, are playfully ironic.

process, *The Americans* became a book that has had a profound influence on scores of today's photographers.

Another photographer whose work has inspired the approach of many modern cameramen and women captured images that were not usually the subject of the camera's eye. Her name was Diane Arbus. She seemed a most unlikely person for producing the kind of photographs she took. A small woman, easily moved to tears, she grew up in a wealthy household in New York City. Yet some of the photographs that brought her fame were of retarded people, of disadvantaged children, and of misshapen men and women who were often cruelly referred to as freaks. Others were of "fringe" people: hippies, transvestites, topless dancers, street people.

Arbus's purpose in taking these pictures was not to demean her subjects. Rather, it was to make viewers pause and reflect upon the fact that they should not take whatever advantages they had in life for granted. Ironically, the images that created the angriest response were those of "normal" people, ordinary middle-class individuals. Her straightforward photographs revealed that most people are blind to how

they really look. They have self-images that to a large extent only they themselves see. "I really believe," she wrote, "there are things which nobody would see unless I photographed them."

Over the years, many people have been disturbed by the content of Arbus's photographs. Some viewers, for example, were upset when her picture of a man and woman who had been awarded the title of king and queen of a senior citizens' ball was published. They felt that Arbus had demeaned the couple by making them look foolish. Others who encountered the photograph, however, praised the image for its honesty. As one critic evaluating Arbus's pictures as a whole has written, "[They are photographs] very difficult to stay out of. . . . What disturbs people more than the subjects of these pictures is the intensity of their power to . . . stop us . . . and ask ourselves who we are."

In an increasingly urbanized world, it is not surprising that the city and those who dwell within it is today one of the most popular of photographic subjects. Among those who have mastered the art of what is commonly referred to as street photography is Lee Friedlander. A dedicated New Yorker, Friedlander has used that city and its inhabitants as a means of exploring the modern human condition. Operating with a 35mm camera, he has obtained many of his pictures by mingling inconspicuously among city crowds and buildings until finding a subject that intrigues him. Some of his favorite subjects have been store windows, monuments and statues, church steeples, city intersections, construction sites, and men and women often lost in thought as if contemplating the realities of city life. Many of his photographs feature reflections of people and objects seen in windows, mirrors, and showcases.

Among Friedlander's most arresting images are the street scenes he has captured. The untitled photograph of a man walking along a sidewalk toward the camera is typical of these pictures. Like almost all Friedlander's street photographs, it is a deliberately informal picture taken on the spur of the moment but rich with informative, expressive elements. The man is surrounded by artifacts of city life—the prominent store sign, the lamp poles, the overhanging streetlights, the automobiles. It is a simple photograph, yet striking in the way it captures the atmosphere of a particular place at a particular time.

In recent decades the world of photography has benefited from the emergence of masterful photographers from countries not previously heralded for their contributions to the medium. In Mexico, for example, three photographers in particular, Graciela Iturbide, Pablo Ortiz Monasterio, and Manuel Alvarez Bravo, have garnered worldwide attention for the quality of their work.

Although Graciela Iturbide has photographed throughout much of Latin

Lee Friedlander. New York street scene, about 1965.

Writing about his photographic experience, Friedlander stated, "I was finding myself at times in the landscape of my photography. I might call myself an intruder. At any rate [my photographs] came about slowly and not with plan but more as another discovery each time."

Alexander Raota. Breaking
horses, about 1985.

*Raota is a modern Argentinean
photographer. His photographs are
marked by a dramatic sense of
action and his ability to portray the
emotions of his subjects.*

America, she has been primarily motivated by a desire to discover the Mexico of her ancestors. She has spent much of her time living among the Indians of her country, documenting their daily lives and customs. Pablo Ortiz Monasterio has been driven by his desire to depict the collision between Mexican values and traditions and the challenges of everyday modern life. His most outstanding work has been accomplished in Mexico City, where he has portrayed the contrasts between old and new and the struggles of the many poor people to maintain their dignity in a metropolis of more than 20 million.

Manuel Alvarez Bravo is widely regarded as the greatest of all Mexican photographers. In a career that has spanned almost seven decades, he has not only produced countless masterful images but is credited with being the inspiration for the accep-

tance and the growth of photography in his native country.

It has been only recently that Alvarez Bravo's work has received the full recognition that it has long deserved. Perhaps that is because, unlike so many photographs noteworthy for their power and dramatic effects, Alvarez Bravo's images are so often subtle, almost hushed in tone. Rather than photograph what might be considered life's most telling moments he has always focused on the much quieter happenings in between. As photohistorian Kathryn Livingston has noted, "Alvarez Bravo's genius lies in seeing the wrinkles of the life around him—the indecisive moment as it were. . . . What he captures best is life in the rests between the notes."

Some of today's photographers have worked in well-established forms of the medium, adding their own special talents and unique vision to take pictures that are as strong as anything that has been done before—even stronger, in the judgment of many people. Such a photographer is the Brazilian photojournalist Sebastião Salgado.

A self-taught photographer, Salgado has spent the last 25 years taking pictures of armed conflict around the globe. He has gained his greatest acclaim thus far, however, through the images that resulted from a huge photographic project he conducted.

In a world where new technology is rapidly replacing old methods of working, Salgado, in the late 1980s and early 1990s, took his camera to many nations to document men and women still involved in manual labor. Published in 1993 in a book titled *Workers,* Salgado's photographs depict such scenes as thousands of laborers toiling with pickaxes and shovels in a Brazilian gold mine (see page 130), other laborers working the sulfur mines of Indonesia, and men digging the Channel Tunnel between England and France. Since their publication, the pictures in *Workers* have been acclaimed as offering a profound commentary on the human condition while, at the same time, providing a powerful tribute to labor.

In the late 1990s Salgado added to his growing reputation through another lengthy photographic project. This time he traveled throughout India and other developing nations to capture unforgettable images of people being dispossessed of their land.

Salgado has proved to be as much at home capturing pictures of individuals and landscapes as he is in recording huge groups of people at work. Perhaps his greatest ability is the way in which, even while photographing scenes of general despair, he is able to portray the dignity of each of the people he photographs.

In contrast to the approach of photographers such as Salgado, many modern photographers have made their mark by continuing the medium's proud tradition of blazing new and imaginative trails. This has been particularly true of Cindy Sherman, who has risen to international fame by producing images that have been termed "true theatre."

In the 1980s Sherman created a sensation when she compiled a series of 69 photographs she called *Untitled Film Stills.* Her

Manuel Alvarez Bravo. *Optical Parable,* 1931.

Bravo's genius can be found in the way he portrays ways of life in a casual yet powerful manner. His messages, wrote one critic, "reach us by slow and continuous flight; little by little they saturate us."

purpose in creating the images was to satirize the stereotypical ways women had long been portrayed in many movies. Sherman appeared in each of the photographs, assuming such roles as a bored housewife, a *femme fatale,* a rebellious teenager, and a victim of abuse. She left it to each viewer to imagine a story line for each picture.

Sherman followed up this provocative series by creating another one titled *History Portraits,* designed once again to call attention to the historic stereotyping of women. This time her subject was the world of art rather than the world of movies. Her purpose was to parody the ways artists from the past had traditionally portrayed women. Once again Sherman appeared in each photograph. She donned various wigs and

dressed herself in the ornate costumes typical of the clothing worn in the portraits she was satirizing.

Sherman's wide acceptance in the general art world is evidenced by the fact that her photographs are included in major collections of such prestigious museums as the Pompidou in Paris, the Museum Folkwang in Essen, Germany, and New York's Museum of Modern Art. As photohistorian Revel Golden has noted, it is a success due to Sherman's unique ability to produce images, that "shock us into reassessing cultural icons that have become so ingrained in daily life we have actually stopped questioning their purpose."

Another of today's highly regarded photographers does not photograph people at

Cindy Sherman. *Untitled Film Still,* 1977.

Sherman is the most prominent feminist photographer, known for images of herself in various assumed roles. Here she is posed as a young innocent in a potentially dangerous situation, perhaps about to be rescued by some hero.

Jerry Uelsmann. *Apocalypse II,*
1967.

*Many of Uelsmann's images were
created not to impart information but
to challenge the viewer to bring his
own thoughts and perceptions to the
picture. This photograph was made by
combining several negatives and
printing them as a single image.*

all. William Wegman (see page 125) concentrates on taking whimsical pictures of dogs, providing us with a delightful example of the way humor has come to be accepted as a legitimate element in seriously conceived photographs.

A graduate of the Massachusetts College of Art, where he studied painting, Wegman turned to photography in 1966. In 1970 two events took place that were to change the course of his career. While attending a party he came across a plate of salami. Fascinated with the small specks of peppercorn on the salami slices, he constructed a photograph, which he titled *Catto,* in which the specks had apparently leapt out of the slices and covered his hand. This image, which launched Wegman into that modern-day whimsical form of photography known as constructed reality, became an instant hit wherever it was shown.

It was in 1970 also that Wegman responded to a newspaper ad for Weimaraner puppies. He named the dog he purchased Man Ray after the innovative American photographer. Little did he know at the time that Weimaraners were to affect his professional life even more dramatically than the success of his *Catto* image.

As Man Ray and a second Weimaraner that Wegman purchased grew older they began repeatedly to wander in front of the camera whenever he was taking a picture. Rather than be upset, Wegman made a bold decision; he would include the dogs in his photographs. It was an inspired move. For more than 25 years Wegman has used a succession of dead-panned, sometimes costumed Weimaraners as the stars of hundreds of images acclaimed not only for their humor but for the more serious, often satirical message the viewer is apt to find in each picture.

From the earliest serious, no-nonsense images of those who sat before the daguerreotype camera to William Wegman's innovative portrayals of his dogs, photography has taken mankind on a journey that has changed the way we view the world. Photography has become the universal language understood by people everywhere.

Photography has become the world's shared experience, involving us emotionally in the triumphs and the tragedies, the joys and sorrows of people throughout the world. It has provided us with an indelible record of who we are, where we've been, and where we seem to be headed.

Because photography has become so much a part of our lives, it is impossible to recount all the ways in which we encounter

Instant Photography

Today we live in a world where taking photographs is the most popular hobby for tens of millions of people around the world. Much of this is due to the way in which modern technology has made picture taking easier than once thought possible. One of the most revolutionary breakthroughs in this modern technology was the creation of the Polaroid Land Camera, created by the American scientist and inventor Dr. Edwin H. Land. The first camera to provide instant prints to the user, the Land Camera first appeared on the market in 1948.

The original Polaroid Land Camera worked this way: A large roll of print paper and a smaller roll of negative paper connected by leaders were loaded into the top and bottom of the camera through the back. After a picture was taken, the photographer pulled on the leader tab that extended through one end of the back. This pulled the print paper and the negative paper together between a pair of rollers. The rollers broke a pod of processing chemicals at one end of the print paper and spread these chemicals evenly between the two papers. After one minute, the finished print could be removed from the camera through a flap in the back. When all the pictures had been taken, the negative roll was discarded and the camera reloaded.

Current Polaroid cameras made for use by amateur photographers feature film packs of individual sheets that combine negative and positive layers and processing chemicals all in a single sheet. When a picture is taken, a motor drive forces the sheet through the rollers and out of a slot in the camera. A color image processes in full light in one to three minutes. There is nothing to discard. Polaroid black-and-white and color films for professional use in large-format cameras have individual peel-apart negative and positive sheets. Some provide a film negative that can be used in an enlarger to make additional prints. There is also a Polaroid color slide film for 35mm cameras.

it. The sporting events and outdoor concerts we attend, for example, are punctuated by the constant flash of cameras. The nature of tourism has changed. Safaris to Africa, for instance, are now enjoyed by travelers armed with cameras rather than guns. Families commonly choose vacation sites based on pictures of a particular spot or area. The badge of the tourist has become the camera draped around the neck.

Ironically, one of the most revealing examples of how prominent a role photography plays in our lives is the occasional controversy it stirs. When, for instance, an exhibition of Robert Mapplethorpe photographs featuring sexually explicit photographs was held, the furor it caused reached all the way to the halls of the United States Congress.

The exhibition became a political issue, with many congressmen demanding that it be closed down and that funding be withdrawn from the National Endowment for the Arts, the government agency that had financed the exhibit. Other congressmen, arguing that art should never be censored, stood behind the exhibition. Throughout

the controversy, the issue was whether or not what might be regarded by some as tasteless or offensive art should be publicly shown. The issue was not whether photography is an art form. That this was taken for granted, even during this emotional debate, is yet another solid indication of how far the acceptance of photography has come.

Technologically, the advances made in photography in recent times have been nothing short of remarkable. Among these has been the perfection and widespread use of inexpensive disposable cameras. Made of plastic with 35mm film sealed within them, disposable cameras come equipped with viewfinders and a built-in flash. Some disposables take panoramic pictures, while others have a built-in zoom lens.

Once all the pictures have been taken, the user takes the camera to a store that develops film. There the film is removed and prints are made. The store sells the used device back to the manufacturer, where the materials are recycled to be used for making new disposable cameras.

The most recent marvel of photography is the digital camera, which captures images electronically on a removable disk or card. As each picture is taken the user can view it on a screen at the back of the camera. The user then inserts the image disk or card into a computer, where the pictures are clearly displayed on the monitor screen. The pictures can be stored for future viewing and can be printed out or e-mailed to family and friends.

Among the most intriguing of all the items introduced into the world of photography has been computer software for working with photographic images. The most widely used such program is called

Robert Rauschenberg.
Retroactive II, 1964.

Rauschenberg is one of a number of artists who have produced compelling collages using a variety of materials, including photographs. Pop artists of the 1960s, such as Andy Warhol, embraced photography as the most popular, or democratic, of all mediums.

Today the ability to use computer software such as PhotoShop to alter the content of photographs allows for the creation of highly imaginative and deceptive images, such as this one by Jann Lipka.

PhotoShop. This innovative software allows a user to manipulate a photograph in almost every way imaginable. Subjects can be rearranged in the picture or deleted completely, while whole new subjects or backgrounds can be added to the image. Colors can be changed. People's heads can be put on the bodies of others. Because PhotoShop makes it so easy to alter a picture, many courts have now ruled photographs to be inadmissible as evidence in legal proceedings.

The pioneers of photography, despite all their contributions, could probably never have imagined that photographs would one day be taken in the far reaches of space or on the depths of the ocean floor. It is unlikely as well that even inventive geniuses such as George Eastman or Eadweard Muybridge could have foreseen the digital camera or PhotoShop. And who among the early innovators could have foreseen that one day, thanks to the technological marvels of communications satellites and the digital system called the Internet, it would be commonplace to send photographs in a matter of seconds from one place to another without leaving one's desk? One thing is for certain. Given all that has taken place, we can be sure that even more remarkable photographic advancements lie ahead.

Chronology

mid 1700s

The camera obscura as a portable box starts to appear, laying the groundwork for the ideas of photography as we know it.

1806

William Hyde Wollaston invents the camera lucida.

1827

Joseph Nicephore Niépce produces a small, crude but permanent image on a metal plate.

1839

Louis Jacques Mandé Daguerre demonstrates the first practical method of recording images with a camera.

1841

William Henry Fox Talbot perfects and patents his calotype process.

Albert Southworth and Joseph Hawes begin taking daguerreotype portraits.

1844

Talbot publishes his *Pencil of Nature.*

1849

Mathew Brady opens his first daguerreotype studio.

1851

Frederick Scott Archer introduces the collodion (wet plate) process.

The first flash equipment, operating with magnesium powder, is introduced.

1853

Roger Fenton begins taking pictures of the Crimean War.

1854

Adolph Eugène Disdéri patents the carte-de-visite.

c.1855

The first cameras for taking stereographic pictures are introduced.

The ferrotype process (tintypes) is introduced to the United States.

1856

Francis Frith begins photographing in the Near East.

1857

Oscar Rejlander begins creating photographs using multiple negatives.

1861

Oliver Wendell Homes perfects the most popular of all devices for viewing stereographic pictures.

James Clerk Maxwell presents the first demonstration of the principles upon which color photography will be based.

1861–65

Mathew Brady and his photographic corps document the Civil War.

1866

Carleton Watkins photographs Yosemite Valley.

1869

Henry Peach Robinson publishes his *Pictorial Effects in Photography.*

1870s

Timothy O'Sullivan and William Henry Jackson photograph the American West.

1871

Richard Leach Maddox introduces the dry plate process.

1872

Eadweard Muybridge captures motion with a camera, through successive frames.

1881

The Eastman Dry Plate Company is founded.

Karl Klic introduces the photogravure process.

1888

George Eastman introduces the Kodak hand-held camera and flexible film.

The halftone printing process is perfected.

1890

Jacob Riis's *How The Other Half Lives* is published.

1891

The Linked Ring is founded in Europe.

Edison develops the motion picture camera utilizing Eastman's flexible film.

1895

Eugène Atget begins to photograph Paris.

1897

Alfred Stieglitz begins publishing *Camera Notes*.

1900

Eastman Kodak's Brownie debuts, selling for $1.00.

1902

The organization known as Photo-Secession is formed in the United States.

1903

Alfred Stieglitz begins publishing *Camera Work*.

1904

The Lumière brothers introduce the autochrome color process.

1907

Edward Curtis begins publishing his 20-volume *The North American Indian*.

1910s

Lewis Hine takes his child labor photographs.

1913

The Leica camera is introduced.

1921

Man Ray creates his first rayogram.

c.1925

László Moholy-Nagy begins creating his photograms.

Photographic transmission by wire or cable is perfected.

1930

The twin-lens Rolleiflex camera is introduced.

1934

Automatic flash equipment is designed for hand-held cameras.

1935

The Farm Security Administration (FSA) photographic project begins.

1936

The first issue of *Life* magazine is published.

1937

Kodachrome color film, developed by Leopold Godowsky and Leopold Mannes, is introduced.

1940

Ansco and Agfa color films are introduced.

1946

Eastman Kodak introduces Ektachrome, the first color film that can be processed by the photographer.

1947

Dr. Edwin Land introduces the first instant print camera, the Polaroid Land Camera.

1955

The Family of Man photographic exhibition begins its long run at New York's Museum of Modern Art.

1959

Robert Frank's *The Americans* is published.

1963

The Kodak Instamatic Camera is introduced.

1966

Flash cubes are introduced.

1969

Astronauts take the first pictures on the moon.

1977

Cindy Sherman begins her photographic series *Untitled Film Stills*.

1987

Both Kodak and Fuji introduce disposable cameras.

1988

Sony and Fuji introduce the first digital cameras for consumer use.

PhotoMac, the first image manipulation program for Macintosh computers, is introduced.

1990

Adobe Photoshop is introduced.

Photography Museums and Websites

Listed below are some of the major museums where you can view photographs taken by recognized masters of photography and those who may be lesser known. By contacting these museums, either by telephone or through their websites, you can find out about current or forthcoming exhibitions.

Some of these places, such as the Library of Congress, have specific collections of photographs on their websites. By logging on to them, you can study the images wherever you have access to a computer.

Note: At www.icom.org/vimp/world.html you will find an online directory of museums throughout the world, organized by country. Another site, www.art4net.com, contains a listing of worldwide photographic exhibitions.

UNITED STATES

Arizona

The Center for Creative Photography
The University of Arizona
1030 North Olive Road
P.O. Box 210103
Tucson, AZ 85721
520-621-7968
www.creativephotography.org

A museum and research center devoted to photography as an art form. The center has a year-long schedule of photographic exhibitions.

California

J. Paul Getty Museum
1200 Getty Center
Los Angeles, CA 90049
310-440-7300
www.getty.edu/museum/

A museum with a huge collection of European and American photographs, the Getty offers a range of special exhibitions.

The Museum of Photographic Arts
1649 El Prado
San Diego, CA 92101
619-238-7559
www.mopa.org

One of the first museums in the country dedicated to the photographic arts. Visitors have the opportunity to view the work of some of the most celebrated photographers in the history of the medium.

District of Columbia

Library of Congress
101 Independence Avenue SE
Washington, DC 20540
202-707-5000
www.loc.gov

The Library of Congress houses one of the largest collections of photographs in the world. Special exhibitions of photographs are held in each of the Library's two main buildings.

Georgia

High Museum of Art
1280 Peachtree Street
Atlanta, GA 30309
404-733-4400
www.high.org

One of the leading museums in the southern United States, this museum has spacious galleries devoted exclusively to the exhibition of the works of both well-known and less familiar photographers.

Heinrich Kühn. *Windblown*, about 1900.
The goal of many pictorialists was to produce photographs that looked as similar to European paintings as possible, such as this image by German photographer Heinrich Kühn.

Illinois

Art Institute of Chicago
111 Michigan Avenue
Chicago, IL 60603
312-443-3600
www.artic.edu

Spanning the history of the medium, this museum's holdings contain images taken by many of the world's most celebrated photographers. Exhibitions of photographs by such masters as Eugène Atget, Paul Strand, and Alfred Stieglitz are regularly held.

Kansas

Spencer Museum of Art
1301 Mississippi Street
University of Kansas
Lawrence, KS 66045
785-864-4710
www.ukans.edu/~sma

The Helen Foresman Spencer Museum of Art is the art museum of the University of Kansas, Lawrence, and has a large photographic collection.

Massachusetts

Museum of Fine Arts, Boston
466 Huntington Avenue
Boston, MA 02115
617-267-9300
www.mfa.org

One of the nation's leading museums, the MFA holds continual exhibitions of the work of photographers ranging from some of the world's first cameramen—and women—to photographers working today.

Michigan

Detroit Institute of Arts
5200 Woodward Avenue
Detroit, MI 48202
313-833-7000
www.dia.org

This institution is the fifth-largest fine arts museum in the United States. Within its more than 100 galleries are several devoted to the exhibition of photography.

Minnesota

Walker Art Center
Vineland Place
Minneapolis, MN 55403
612-375-7600
www.walkerart.org/jsindex.html

The Walker Art Center is known for its major exhibitions of 20th-century art, multidisciplinary approach, and innovative education programs.

Missouri

Nelson-Atkins Museum of Art
4525 Oak Street
Kansas City, MO 64111
816-751-1278
www.nelson-atkins.org

One of the country's premier art institutions, this museum's holdings range from the beginnings of photography to the present, including a large collection of Francis Frith prints of Egypt.

Saint Louis Art Museum
Forest Park
St. Louis, MO 63110
314-721-0072
www.slam.org

Housing works by photographers from all periods of the medium, this museum is known for the quality of the special photographic exhibitions it regularly holds.

New York

George Eastman House/ International Museum of Photography
900 East Avenue
Rochester, NY 14607
716-271-3361
www.eastman.org

The George Eastman House's photographic collection is justifiably regarded as one of the most comprehensive in the world. Just as George Eastman revolutionized photography, this museum that bears his name has revolutionized the world of photographic exhibitions.

The International Center of Photography (ICP)
1133 Avenue of the Americas
New York, NY 10036
212 860-1777
www.icp.org

The International Center of Photography is a museum with changing exhibits, a school, and a center for photographers and photography. Each year, ICP presents the Infinity Awards for excellence in photography, one of the most prestigious photographic awards.

Metropolitan Museum of Art
1000 Fifth Avenue
New York, NY 10028
212-879-5500
www.metmuseum.org

Founded in 1870, the "Met," as it is fondly called, is one of the finest museums in the world. Its photographic collection and exhibitions have long been acclaimed worldwide.

Museum of Modern Art

11 West 53rd Street
New York, NY 10019
212-708-9400
www.moma.org

A pioneer in mounting photographic shows, this museum, known as MOMA. was the site of the historic 1955 "Family of Man" exhibition.

Whitney Museum of American Art

945 Madison Avenue
New York, NY 10021
212-570-3676
www.whitney.org

The Whitney, founded by Gertrude Vanderbilt Whitney, houses one of the world's foremost collections of 20th-century American art. It holds regular photographic exhibitions.

Ohio

Cleveland Museum of Art

University Circle
11150 East Boulevard
Cleveland, OH 44106
216-421-7340
www.clemusart.com

Collections at this museum span from ancient Egypt to works of contemporary art. Its photography department mounts permanent, temporary, and traveling exhibitions.

Pennsylvania

Philadelphia Museum of Art

26th Street & Benjamin Franklin Parkway
Philadelphia, PA 19130
215-763-8100
www.philamuseum.org

Among the largest art museums in the United States, it has one of the nation's oldest photographic collections and holds regular exhibitions of both old and new works.

Texas

Amon Carter Museum

3501 Camp Bowie Boulevard
Fort Worth, TX 76107
817-736-1933
www.cartermuseum.org

Specializing in all aspects of American art, the Amon Carter houses the work of scores of American photographers.

Dallas Museum of Art

1717 North Harwood Street
Dallas, TX 75201
214-922-1200
www.dm-art.org

This museum has many programs designed especially for young people. It holds both permanent and temporary photographic collections.

Harry Ransom Humanities Research Center

P.O. Box 7219
Austin, TX 78713
512-471-9124
www.hrc.utexas.edu/

The Ransom Center at the University of Texas is an interdisciplinary archive and museum that holds more than 5 million original prints and negatives, including the first photograph ever taken, by Joseph

Nicephore Niépce. It has regular photographic exhibitions.

Washington

Seattle Art Museum

100 University Street
Seattle, WA 98101
206-654-3100
www.seattleartmuseum.org

One of the most user-friendly museums in the nation, it complements its exhibitions with films and lectures.

AUSTRALIA

Australian Center for Photography

257 Oxford Street
Paddington, NSW, 2021
Sydney, Australia 02 9332 1455
www.acp.au.com

The mission of the center is to "promote and enrich the understanding of photo-based art in Australia" through exhibitions, education, and publications. It houses exhibition spaces, an extensive workshop, and a research library.

CANADA

Glenbow Museum

130 Ninth Avenue SE
Calgary, Alberta T2G OP3
Canada
403-266-4100
www.glenbow.org

The Glenbow is a museum, art gallery, library, and archive, all of which focus on the human history of Canada's Northwest. It features exhibitions of work by Canadian photographers throughout the history of the medium.

National Gallery of Canada
380 Sussex Drive
P.O. Box 427, Station A
Ottawa, Ontario K1N 9N4
Canada
613-990-1985
www.national.gallery.ca

This museum features regular exhibitions of works by Canadian cameramen and women, as well as photographs from European and American photographers.

Vancouver Art Gallery
750 Hornby Street
Vancouver, British Columbia V6Z 2H71
Canada
604-662-4700
www.vanartgallery.bc.ca
Featuring the work of Canadian photographers, this museum holds both permanent and temporary exhibitions.

Justina M. Barnicke Gallery
Hart House
7 Hart House Circle
University of Toronto
Toronto, Ontario M5S 3H3
416-978-8398
www.utoronoto.ca/gallery

Although specializing in images captured by Canadian masters of the medium, this gallery regularly displays the work of photographers from around the world.

ENGLAND

The Fox Talbot Museum
Lacock, Chippenham
Wiltshire SN15 2LG
England
44 1249 730 459

Located inside a 15th-century barn, this museum commemorates the life and work of William Henry Fox Talbot. It holds exhibitions of a broad range of work by contemporary and 19th-century photographers.

Imperial War Museum
Lambeth Road
London SE1 6HZ
England
44 207 416 5320
www.iwm.org.uk

This museum is dedicated to an understanding of the history of modern war and "wartime experience." It has a comprehensive collection of photographs taken from World War I to the present day and holds regular exhibitions of war photography.

National Museum of Photography, Film & Television
Bradford
West Yorkshire BD1 1NQ
England
44 1274 20 20 30

Founded in 1983 as part of the National Museum of Science and Industry, it holds an impressive photographic collection, including the world's first negative, created by William Henry Fox Talbot.

Victoria and Albert Museum
Cornwall Road
South Kensington
London SW7 2RL
England
44 207 942 2000
www.vwm.ac.uk

One of the most renowned museums in the world, the Victoria and Albert contains 146 galleries. The works of masters of British photography are regularly exhibited at the museum.

FRANCE

La Maison Européenne de la Photographie
82 rue François Miron
75 004 Paris
France
33 1 44 78 75 00
www.mep-fr.org/us/default.htm

The permanent collection of the European House of Photography consists of more than 15,000 images and is representative of international photography from the end of the 1950s to the present.

JAPAN

National Museum of Modern Art
3 Kitanomaru Koen
Chiyoda-Tokyo 102-8322
Japan
813-3214-2561
813-3272-8600 Information service
www.momat.go.jp

The National Museum of Modern Art was opened in 1952 as Japan's first national art museum. Along with works by photographers from many nations, its exhibitions feature images taken by acclaimed Japanese photographers.

Tokyo Metropolitan Museum of Photography
1-13-3 Mita
Meguro-ku
Tokyo 153-0062
Japan
813-3280-0031
www.tokyo-photo—museum.or.jp

The exhibits and photographic holdings of this museum are primarily by Japanese photographers.

Further Reading

General Histories of Photography

Beaton, Cecil, and Gail Buckland. *The Magic Image: The Genius of Photography from 1839 to the Present Day*. London: Weidenfeld and Nicolson, 1975.

Frizot, Mitchel, Colin Harding, and Pierre Albert, eds. *A New History of Photography*. New York: Könemann, 1998.

George Eastman House. *Photography from George Eastman House, Rochester, NY*. New York: Taschen, 1999.

Goldberg, Vicki, and Robert Silberman. *American Photography: A Century of Images*. San Francisco: Chronicle, 1999.

Newhall, Beaumont. *The History of Photography: From 1839 to the Present*. 5th rev. ed. New York: Museum of Modern Art, 1982.

Rosenblum, Naomi. *A World History of Photography*. New York: Abbeville, 1997.

Sandler, Martin W. *America, A Celebration!* New York: Dorling Kindersley, 2000.

———. *American Image: Photographing One Hundred Fifty Years in the Life of a Nation*. Chicago: Contemporary Books, 1989.

———. *The Story of American Photography: An Illustrated History for Young People*. New York: Little, Brown, 1979.

Stepan, Peter, ed. *Icons of Photography: The Twentieth Century*. New York: Prestel, 1999.

Szarkowski, John. *Looking at Photographs: 100 Pictures from the Collection of the Museum of Modern Art*. Greenwich, Conn.: New York Graphic Society, 1973.

Aspects or Periods of Photography

Darrah, William C. *The World of Stereographs*. Gettysburg, Pa.: William C. Darrah, 1977.

Eastman Kodak Company. *The Joy of Photography*. Reading, Mass.: Addison-Wesley, 1991.

Eauclaire, Sally. *The New Color Photography*. New York: Abbeville, 1981.

Finn, David. *How to Look at Photographs: Reflections on the Art of Seeing*. New York: Abrams, 1994.

Fleming, Paula Richardson, and Judith Luskey. *The North American Indians in Photographs*. New York: Harper & Row, 1986.

John T. Daniels. Flight of the Wright brothers, 1903.

Taken at the moment when the Wright brothers achieved the long-sought-after conquest of manned flight, Daniels's image was one of the earliest published photographs to have a significant effect on the viewing public. It provided visual evidence of a miracle of its age.

Goldberg, Vicki, ed. *Photographs in Print: Writings from 1816 to the Present.* New York: Simon & Schuster, 1988.

Greenhill, Ralph. *Early Photography in Canada.* Toronto: Oxford University Press, 1965.

Guggenheim Museum. *In/Sight, African Photographers, 1940 to the Present.* New York: Abrams, 1996.

Haworth-Booth, Mark. *The Golden Age of British Photography 1839–1900: Photographs from the Victoria and Albert Museum with Selections from the Philadelphia Museum of Art . . . .* New York: Aperture, 1984.

Hurley, F. Jack. *Industry and the Photographic Image: 153 Great Prints from 1850 to the Present.* New York: Dover, 1980.

Margolis, Marriane Fulton, ed. *Camera Work: A Pictorial Guide.* New York: Dover, 1978.

Meredith, Roy. *Mr. Lincoln's Camera Man: Mathew B. Brady.* 2d rev. ed. New York: Dover, 1974.

Newhall, Beaumont. *The Daguerreotype in America.* 3rd rev. ed. New York: Dover, 1976.

Peterson, Christian A. *Alfred Stieglitz's Camera Notes.* New York: Norton, 1993.

Rosenblum, Naomi. *A History of Women Photographers.* New York: Abbeville, 1994.

Stryker, Roy Emerson, and Nancy Wood. *In This Proud Land: America as Seen in the FSA Photographs.* Boston: New York Graphic Society,1973.

Sullivan, Constance, ed. *Great Photographic Essays from* Life. Boston: New York Graphic Society, 1978.

Willis, Deborah. *Reflections in Black: A History of Black Photographers, 1840 to the Present.* New York: Norton, 2000.

Wood, John, and Merry A. Foresta. *The Art of the Autochrome: The Birth of Color Photography.* Iowa City: University of Iowa Press, 1993.

Individual Photographers

Alinder, James, and John Szarkowski. *Ansel Adams: Classic Images.* Boston: Little, Brown, 1986.

Callahan, Sean, ed. *The Photography of Margaret Bourke-White.* Boston: New York Graphic Society, 1975.

Daniel, Pete, and Raymond Smock. *A Talent for Detail: The Photographs of Miss Frances Benjamin Johnston, 1889–1910.* New York: Harmony, 1974.

Ford, Colin, ed. *An Early Victorian Album: The Photographic Masterpieces (1843–1847) of David Octavius Hill and Robert Adamson.* New York: Knopf, 1976.

Frank, Robert. *The Americans.* New York: Pantheon, 1986.

Frank, Waldo, et al., eds. *America and Alfred Stieglitz: A Collective Portrait.* Millerton, N.Y.: Aperture, 1979.

Frith, Francis. *Egypt and the Holy Land in Historic Photographs.* New York: Dover, 1980.

Gernsheim, Helmut. *Julia Margaret Cameron, Her Life and Photographic Work.* 2d. ed. Millerton, N.Y.: Aperture, 1975.

Hurley, F. Jack. *Marion Post Wolcott: A Photographic Journey.* Albuquerque: University of New Mexico Press, 1989.

Jones, Edgar. *Father of Art Photography: O. G. Rejlander, 1813–1875.* Greenwich, Conn.: New York Graphic Society, 1973.

Karsh, Yusuf. *Karsh: A Sixty-Year Retrospective.* Boston: Bullfinch, 1996.

Maddox, Ben. *Edward Weston, His Life and Photographs: The Definitive Volume of His Photographic Work.* Millerton, N.Y.: Aperture, 1979.

Metzger, Jerald C., intro. *Walker Evans: Photographs for the Farm Security Administration.* New York: Da Capo, 1973.

Michaels, Barbara L. *Gertrude Käsebier: The Photographer and Her Photographs.* New York: Abrams, 1992.

Millstein, Barbara Head, and Sarah M. Lowe. *Consuela Kanaga: An American Photographer.* Brooklyn, N.Y.: Brooklyn Museum, 1992.

Newhall, Nancy. *P. H. Emerson: The Fight for Photography as a Fine Art.* New York: Aperture, 1975.

Plimpton, George, intro. *Toni Frissell, Photographs: 1933–1967.* New York: Doubleday, 1994.

Sobieszek, Robert A., and Odette M. Appel. *The Daguerreotypes of Southworth and Hawes.* New York: Dover, 1980.

Steichen, Edward. *The Family of Man: The Photographic Exhibition.* New York: Simon & Schuster, 1955.

———. *A Life in Photography.* Garden City, N.Y.: Doubleday, 1981.

Trachtenberg, Alan. *America and Lewis Hine: Photographs 1904–1940.* New York: Aperture, 1977.

Index

Page references in **boldface** type refer to illustrations.

Workers in the early 1900s assembling the Number 4A Folding Kodak camera, considered to be the ancestor of all modern folding roll cameras.

This photograph of an American family was left behind on the lunar surface as evidence of man's visit to the moon.

Picture Credits

Acknowledgments

It would not be possible to compile a book of this nature without the help of many individuals. I am once again deeply grateful to Thurman (Jack) Naylor, owner of one of the world's most complete private photographic museums and collections. Jack's generosity in allowing so many of the unique images in his possession to be used in this book and the technical knowledge he has shared with me have been invaluable.

I would also like to thank Jesse Johnson of the Photoduplication Department of the Library of Congress for her prompt responses to my requests and questions and Ulrich Figge for his photographic genius. As always, Carol Sandler typed all of the several drafts of this book without complaint and provided valuable suggestions all along the way. I regret that space does not allow me to extend my deep gratitude individually to the curators and staff members of the many institutions from which the photographs in this book were obtained. Please accept my blanket thanks.

Finally, I have had the great fortune of having Lisa Barnett as my editor. If I have accomplished what I set out to do in this book, it is because of her superior editing skills, her help in shaping the volume, and her refusal to allow us to compromise on finding "just the right photograph."

About the Author

Martin W. Sandler is the author of forty-one books, two of which have been nominated for the Pulitzer Prize. His *Story of American Photography: An Illustrated History for Young People* received The Horn Book Award in 1984. Sandler's other books include *America, A Celebration!*, *The Vaqueros: The World's First Cowmen*, and a Library of Congress American History series for young adults. An accomplished television producer and writer as well, Sandler has received Emmy and Golden Cine awards for his television series and programs on history, photography, and American business. He has taught American Studies to students in junior high and high school, as well as at the University of Massachusetts and Smith College. He lives in Cotuit, Massachusetts, with his wife Carol.